D1582938

Roland and Sabrina Michaud

Mirror of India

With 175 colour illustrations

Thames and Hudson

To Our Mother India

Designed by Sabrina Michaud

Introduction translated from the French
by Ruth Sharman
Notes on the Plates translated from the French
by Emily Lane

First published in Great Britain in 1990
by Thames and Hudson Ltd, London

Printed and bound in France

And always, from the depths of millions of eyes, we meet the look of the One

Romain Rolland

(from the Preface to Ananda Coomaraswamy's *The Dance of Siva*)

It is 1985 and we are behind the scenes in London's Victoria and Albert Museum, admiring a number of 16th-century Mughal miniatures. One in particular catches our eye. It depicts the Emperor Akbar watching a scuffle between two rival groups of *sadhus* or holy men. We marvel at the picture's quasi-photographic realism, at the extraordinarily fine detail produced by the squirrel-hair brush.

We had been regular visitors to India for the last twenty years, and yet we had never witnessed such a scene in reality. We could only dream about it and wonder if there was the remotest chance of our seeing, with our own eyes, anything like that in India today.

Four years later, on Monday 6 February 1989, the day of the new moon during the month of Magha, we were in Allahabad for the Great Kumbha Mela. Perched on a police observation platform, surrounded by a seething mass of humanity, we had come to witness India's holiest bathing festival. This major religious event, which takes place once every twelve years, attracts the largest single gathering of people in the world.

What is more, according to astrologers the stars had not been so auspiciously constellated for 144 years – suggesting that a whole multitude of divine favours might be forthcoming! As a result, fifteen million pilgrims had come to wash away their sins in the Sangam, the confluence of three holy rivers: the Ganges, the Yamuna, and the Saraswati, celebrated in Hindu mythology.

Just a few days before, the *sadhus* of the Nirmanjani order had accused those of the Juna order of setting fire to their campsite, and it was only through the hasty intervention of the police that the two groups were prevented from coming to blows. On that festival Monday, there was a feeling that the merest spark could touch off the powder-keg.

As the sun fired the Indian earth, we had the sense of being party to something truly epic. Two thousand naked *sadhus* swarmed in the direction of the Sangam, as if rushing to confront an enemy; brandishing swords and tridents, intoxicated by a night of smoking, these warriors of Shiva seemed to have stepped straight out of the pages of the *Mahabharata*. The atmosphere of tension and excitement was extraordinary. For a moment, we were transformed into Akbar himself...

In India, there is no division between art and life. In contrast to Egyptian, Greek and Chinese traditions, Indian tradition is a living thing, and it is this vitality that we have sought to demonstrate in this book. By drawing on two modes of visual expression – the painting or sculpture and the photograph – it is our intention to highlight the dazzling multiplicity of Indian culture from two complementary perspectives. And by evoking the symmetrical interplay between the best elements of the past and the best of the present, we aim to show how past and present enrich one another and ultimately merge.

More often than not, years separate the discovery of the painted or carved scene from that of the living one. When recording images in museums and libraries, we were not to know that these same images would one day assume a living form. In the course of our wanderings, we photographed things that caught our eye, unaware that these same scenes had provided the inspiration for famous miniaturists. Such encounters between art and life always have a miraculous quality about them. We did battle for each and every image, consumed by our passion for the project. Ever on the lookout, we cast our nets wide, determined to capture that something that outlasts the moment, and each success was like a drop of honey in a sea of mud. Shouldering aside ugliness, obstacles and indifference, we gradually assembled the scattered pieces of this puzzle which is many-mirrored India.

India has been the source of our inspiration for the past twenty-five years. On our first trip, in 1965, we sensed already that the works of art which emanated from Indian culture reflected a very particular reality. As our planet becomes increasingly standardized, that reality may well be as bleak as any other, but it continues to encapsulate an essence of such richness that we feel compelled to bear witness to it. Reaching beyond the outward forms, it is this essence that we are for ever striving to penetrate.

To understand any foreign culture requires a key. In our view, this key is to be found in a knowledge of symbols, which, by their universality, have the power to affect us irrespective of cultural differences. Originally the word symbol (from the Greek *sumbolon*) signified an object cut into two, each part constituting an identifying marker enabling it to be reunited (*sumballein*) with the other.

According to this definition, the symbol permits a perception of a global whole, the opening up of a reality perceived in an intuitive and synthesizing fashion, one in which objects are brought together in a unity which transcends them. The symbol reveals the correspondences between things and, via the springboard of myth, allows us to penetrate to the archetype. To photographers (and, what is more, to photographers in this Indian universe where the eye is assaulted – alternatively bewildered, terrified and enchanted – by the vast quantities of raw material that confront it on all sides) what symbol could have seemed more apposite than the mirror?

Over and beyond its primary function – faithful reproduction of the object – the mirror becomes an instrument of knowledge. Its role is to confirm the response to our own questions. Once the shock of the raw image has passed, it is then a matter of refining, by means of this instrument, what the eye sees; of understanding by means of the reflection; ultimately of knowing by means of the mirror. Sharpening our eye, honing our sensibilities, the mirror is the magic key which opened the door for us to an under-standing of India.

In the Hindu world view, the gods are archetypes which we humans endeavour to imitate. By their very nature, these archetypes are the models upon which the various aspects of the perceptible universe are based. Man is able to perceive his own existence only in so far as it is a reflection of the divine.

Every Indian man recognizes himself in Krishna, Rama or Shiva, and in each Indian woman there is a Radha, a Sita or a Parvati. An aspect of the divine may be represented and worshipped in the most varied forms, such as a sculpture or an image (*murti*), an individual human being, a master (*guru*), even a tree, a rock, or an animal; and each of these forms may be employed as a prop to aid in the attainment, through ritual and meditation, of the principle of which they are the outward manifestation.

In this quest, which adopts the most unusual guises, the function of sight is traditionally pre-eminent. The image does not only offer possibilities for concentration: it is a personification of the divine. To see is to know and, according to the *Brahmanas*, the eye equals truth.

India's culture is visual. So intrigued is it by the eye that it has gone so far as to invent a third. Each of us is thought to have one: situated in the middle of the forehead just above the juncture between the brows, and the centre of powerful occult energies. Symbol of magic vision, this third eye is an attribute of the *yogi*, India's master magician, and is associated with the god Shiva.

In a memorable episode from Hindu mythology, Shiva is playing games with his consort Parvati in their Himalayan home and as a joke Parvati suddenly covers Shiva's eyes with her hands; the world is plunged into darkness, and, in order to rescue it from such an undesirable state of affairs, Shiva creates an eye in the middle of his forehead. The symbolism of this third eye, alternately regarded as benevolent and baleful, is as rich as it is complex. It is represented by the red dot, known as the *tilak*, which married women paint in the middle of their forehead. The symbol of Parvati's awareness following her initiation by Shiva, the *tilak* also serves as a protective mark placed by the *pujaris* – temple guardians and officiants –

on the forehead of visitors and pilgrims. It is traditionally believed that the gods distinguish one another from mortals by the fact that their eyes never blink.

The Indian goes to the temple to see, and to be seen by, God. Great importance is attributed to this notion of seeing – *darshana* – since it is thought that through this mutual contemplation the worshipper develops his or her awareness. It is for this reason that India as a whole functions as one huge pilgrimage site. Its pilgrims go from holy place to holy place in order to gaze on the famous temple images, and to receive the blessing that contemplation of these images confers. In the same way, vast crowds travel to receive the *darshana* (*darshana lena*, 'take sight') of a living person whom they revere and who in turn gives them his *darshana* (*darshana denta*).

Darshana and worship are two essential aspects of religious life in India. On a day-to-day basis, the image of the deity is kept concealed from view; it is only made visible at certain times, when the curtain veiling the *murti* is drawn back so that the pilgrim may look into its eyes. In preparation for this privileged moment, the deity is robed, painted and perfumed so as to appear to the pilgrim in all the perfection of its divine beauty, thus increasing the chances of success of this visual communion.

At Nathdwara, in Rajasthan, an image of Shrinathji – the manifestation of the god Krishna at the age of seven – is the focus for intense activity on the part of the whole town. For his devotees, come from the four corners of India, this representation of Shrinathji is truly living, to the point that it is housed in its own dwelling, or *haveli*, rather than in the temple itself. Everything is done to please Shrinathji and to ensure that he lacks for nothing. In summer, the figure is clothed in a simple *dhoti*, or loincloth, and the air above its head is kept constantly stirred by a hand-held peacock-feather fan. In winter, the figure is dressed in a quilted coat to shield it from the cold. To satisfy its hunger, the most succulent delicacies are specially prepared, and to slake its thirst, water is brought from the holy Yamuna, hundreds of miles distant. In the evening, care is even taken to ensure that Shrinathji's flute is not within his reach, since it is believed that if he takes it into his head to play this instrument in the early hours, his listeners will be so entranced that none will go to work. The number of officiants entrusted with these various tasks runs into thousands. Eight times a day, the sanctuary is open for the *darshana*, during which worshippers are permitted to gaze for a few moments on the divine god-child – a spiritual experience that can lead to enlightenment.

In 1990, during a trip down the Narmada – one of the holiest of all rivers, since the mere sight of it is said to purify the heart – I observed a scene that gave me pause for thought. At Bhera Ghat (Marble Rocks), in the Temple of the Sixty-Four Yoginis, the *pujari* was busy attending to a *murti* representing Shankar and Gauri (variants of Shiva and Parvati) as a married couple astride the bull Nandi. Every day, from five to ten in the morning, he attended with meticulous care to the toilet of the divine couple and, with the *darshana* in mind, lovingly dwelt on the tiniest details of their appearance. They received a change of clothes; fresh flowers were placed on their heads; and the *tilak* was painted on with sandalwood paste which the *pujari* prepared fresh each day. Imagine, then, my astonishent when, one day, I caught a glimpse of the old man placing a little mirror in the palm of his hand and offering it to the god and goddess in turn! It was a fleeting scene – over in a matter of seconds – but the moment filled me with a strange sense of elation: it was not a matter now of reading or research but of my own eyes, and through what I had seen I was able to understand.

In India, the function of seeing is so important that when images of the gods are made the eyes are sculpted, painted in or placed in position last of all, only after the *murti* has received the breath of life (*prana*). For the Indians have quite rightly noted that the eye is the only physical organ whose function begins after birth. The ritual opening of the image's eyes is accomplished by means of a gold needle or a final brushstroke, and the first thing upon which their gaze falls should be agreeable and beautiful; that is why, for this 'sighting' ceremony, a mirror is frequently placed before the new-born deity.

If the *darshana* involves an exchange between deity and worshipper via the intermediary of the eyes, this is because the various traditions agree that it is by contemplating divine perfection that the worshipper himself becomes perfect. The fact that the deity as fashioned by human hands is inherently imperfect presents no paradox; the image merely represents the perfect beauty of the divine, and the faith of the believer will re-create that perfection within his own mind.

Access to knowledge depends, therefore, on seeing. The word 'knowledge' is understood here in the sense of 'consciousness' or 'awareness', that is, man's faculty for knowing his own reality. Having accepted that this essential reality is divine, by contemplating and worshipping the image of the divine – in the mirror which the god holds out to him – the Indian seeks to penetrate to an awareness of divinity within himself.

This is where all the implications of that reflective interplay between worshipper and image as aid to contemplation receive their full force. The notion of the mirror as an instrument of knowledge links the term 'contemplation' (*speculatio*) with the word 'mirror' (*speculum*) itself; and yet the instrument, or aid, is clearly not enough in itself to bring the worshipper to a consciousness of the divine essence. As a prerequisite to such consciousness, the 'inner mirror' of the believer, that mirror in which is reflected the image of perfection as perceived by the eye, must itself be perfect. The quality of the *darshana* ultimately depends on the quality of the believer's faith – or, put another way, on the transparency of his vision.

Sufi masters use the same symbol when instructing their disciples that the heart of man is blind and impure, comparing this heart to a tarnished mirror that must be polished if it is to reflect the rays of the divine sun. This polishing is made possible by invoking the name of God, or Allah – a practice that employs a different prop but has the same end in view.

Thus, it appears not only that the mirror answers us according to the degree of our understanding, but also that the answer is as much in the mirror itself as in the eyes of the beholder. An anecdote taken from the famous Arab myth of Leila and Majnun illustrates the point. 'Majnun' is literally translated as 'Fool' and the Persians have made him into the symbol of unconditional love, whereby they understand a love that transcends human (Leila's) beauty to embrace the beauty that is divine.

Harun had heard people speak of Majnun's love for Leila and was eager to set eyes on this famous beauty. So he summoned Leila to him, but when he saw her found nothing extraordinarily lovely about her. Then he sent for Majnun and said to him: 'This Leila whose beauty has turned your head isn't so very beautiful after all.' And Majnun replied: 'Leila's beauty is flawless; it is your eyes that are at fault. To see her beauty, you need Majnun's eyes.'

The story told to us by Jalal ud-din Rumi in his *Mathnawi* (Distichs) provides a further elaboration:

One day, a sultan called a number of painters to his palace. Some of them were from China, others from Byzantium. The Chinese were convinced that they were the better artists, and the Greeks thought of themselves likewise. So the sultan organized a competition as a means of deciding between them, entrusting them with the task of painting frescoes on two facing walls of his palace. A curtain was hung between the competitors to prevent them being influenced by one another. Whereas the Chinese used a whole range of colours and painted their frescoes with all the intricacy and skill of which they were capable, the Greeks merely spent the time endlessly smoothing and polishing their wall. At the end of the competition, when the sultan came to judge the work, he was fired with enthusiasm for the Chinese frescoes. Then the curtain was drawn back: the sultan saw the magnificent frescoes all over again reflected on the opposite wall, which shone like a mirror; but everything that the sultan had seen on the Chinese side seemed to him much more beautiful as reflected on the wall of the Greeks.

The author goes on to explain:

The Greeks are the Sufis: they are not interested in studying and reading books and accumulating knowledge. But they have polished their hearts and cleansed them of greed, lust and hatred. This clear, untarnished mirror is undoubtedly the heart that receives the imprint of innumerable images.

Here, then, is a symbol common to two quite separate cultures. The miniature in Plate 128 represents the Muslim saint Sarmad, a Jewish Armenian merchant who converted to Islam, then gave up all his worldly goods on the strength of a mystical experience and wandered naked throughout India, where he was nevertheless received as the guest of kings. Opposite him is a Vaishnavite sage, Master One Thousand and Eight, photographed in his tent at the camp of the *bairagis* (Vaishnavite *sadhus*) on the occasion of the world's most important religious festival. More than three centuries separate our photograph from the miniature of Sarmad. Sarmad was a Muslim; his mirror is a Hindu. By setting them side by side, it is our intention to show what unites these two religious men beyond their cultural differences, beyond Hinduism and Islam: the presence of a spirit which transcends the limitations of the form in which it is incarnated. Here, where the image and its reflection are united, the mirror teaches us that it is possible to see beyond the form and catch a glimpse of the essence.

The symbol of the mirror abounds throughout India and is so richly represented that it would be futile to attempt to give a comprehensive overview of it here. Let us consider one particular sculpture that can be seen on the façades of innumerable temples: the one that represents a woman gazing at her reflection in a mirror (Plate 147). For a long time we were perplexed by the significance of such an activity in such a context, but it is perfectly clear to us today that what we are witnessing here is not simply a woman at her toilet. The image can equally well be interpreted as the contemplation of our essential being. It is not her own image that the sculpted heroine is contemplating, but that of her Creator in one of that Creator's multiple forms, of which we are each of us a manifestation.

If the interpretation is taken a stage further, the mirror, as a reflecting surface for all manifest forms of the divine, becomes the symbol itself of the unmanifest, of that which is hidden. In *The Speaking Tree*, Richard Lannoy refers to the ceremony of the Night Watch – *attala puja* – which takes place every evening in the temple of Shuchindram, near Cape Comorin. A procession wends its way through the corridors, which are lit by thousands of oil lamps, paying homage to each of the deities that occupy the thirty-odd temple altars. The climax of the ceremony occurs when the high priest enters a sanctuary that is entirely bare but for a mirror symbolizing the unmanifested aspect of Shiva and, standing before this mirror, worships his own reflection. It is thought that anyone who sees his own image reflected in the mirror has attained union with the One.

Art is an exercise of self-discipline. Even though he knew the story well, Valmiki prepared himself for the task of composing his *Ramayana* by practising yoga until he was able to see its heroes living and breathing before his very eyes. His is an example we have always sought to keep in mind.

Even in photography it is not simply a question of faithfully reproducing the multiple aspects of existence, but of embracing as fully as possible the mental image we form of them. We have at last gathered together all our Indian mirrors. The mirror has helped us reflect (from the Latin *reflectere*, 'to emit back by reflection'), so that we in our turn may act as reflectors.

As a child, Rama, the seventh avatar of Vishnu, had such a fervent desire to possess the moon that nothing anyone offered him could appease his longing – until someone put a mirror into his hand.

Such is the symmetry between reality and illusion that the boundary between them remains imperceptible. Through time and space, this confrontation between the two continues to amaze us.

Finally, the value of the mirror resides in its mystery. It is the place where the 'other side' remains for ever hidden, since to find it would require that we pass right through the mirror.

Divine beauty is in all things. Vaishnavite Hindus call God Bhuvanasundara, 'the Universally Beautiful', and Muslims claim 'God is Beautiful and loves Beauty' – the two major religions of India, one the oldest in the world, the other the youngest, thus reflecting one another in the same Truth.

Roland and Sabrina Michaud

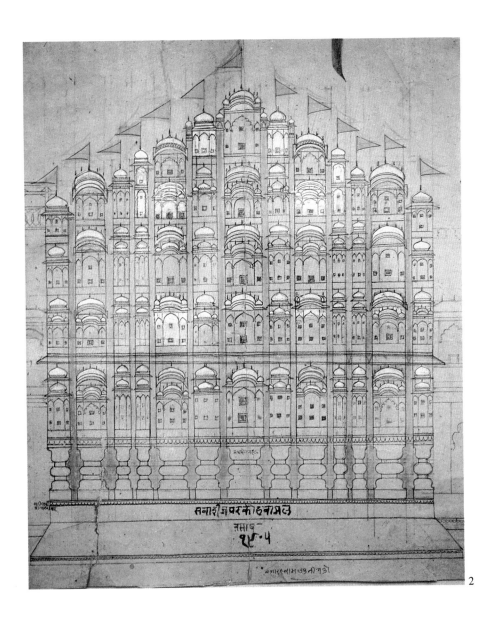

3

4

5

7

10

11

14

15

16

18

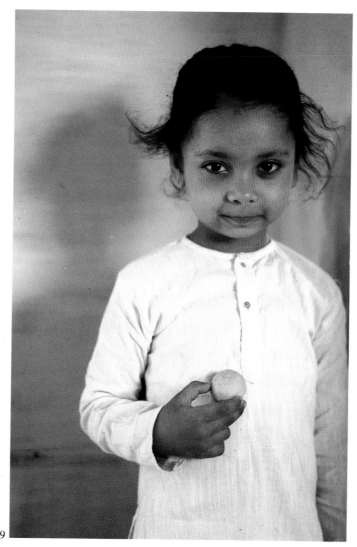

19

'Bring me a fig from that banyan tree.'
'Here is one, father.'
'Open it.'
'Here, it is cut open.'
'What do you see?'
'Very tiny seeds, father.'
'Cut open one of them.'
'Here, it is cut open.'
'What do you see?'
'Nothing, father.'
'My dear boy! This nothing which you do not perceive,
that huge tree has sprung up from it.
My dear boy, you must believe!
This very nothing is self to all that exists.
That is reality. That is self.
And that you are, my son!'

Chândogya Upanishad 6.12. 1-2

21

22

23

33

34

36

If someone says to you:
'In the fortified city of the imperishable,
our body, there is a lotus
and in this lotus a tiny space:
what does it contain that one
should desire to know it?'

You must reply:
'As vast as this space without
is the tiny space within your heart:
heaven and earth are found in it,
fire and air, sun and moon,
lightning and the constellations,
whatever belongs to you here below
and all that doesn't,
all this is gathered in that tiny space
within your heart.'

Chândogya Upanishad 8.1, 2-3

38

39

40

41

42

44

45

46

47

48

49

51

53

58

59

You are woman, you are man.
You are the youth and the maiden too.
You are the old man tottering on his staff.
Once born you take on all forms.
You are the dark-blue bird,
and the green parrot with red eyes,
the cloud pregnant with lightning.
You are the seasons and the seas.
Having no beginning you are everywhere,
you from whom all worlds are born.

Shvetâshvatara Upanishad 4, 1-4

61

63

64

66

69

75

78

The self is the bridge
that holds these two different worlds apart.
Day nor night can cross it, nor old age, nor death,
nor suffering, nor good or bad deeds.

On crossing this bridge the blind is no longer blind,
the wounded no longer wounded and the sick no longer sick.
Whosoever crosses this bridge,
for him night turns into day.

Chândogya Upanishad 8.4, 1-2

83

84

87

88

89

90

93

Just as people,
not knowing that a treasure is hidden in the field,
pass over it day after day without ever finding it,
so do these creatures live day after day
without ever finding the self within their heart.

Chândogya Upanishad 8.3, 2

99

101

104

105

107

109

The self-existent pierced the openings outwards,
therefore does one look without not within.
Some sage in search of immortality
turned back his gaze and saw the self.

Katha Upanishad 4, 1

115

120

123

124

127

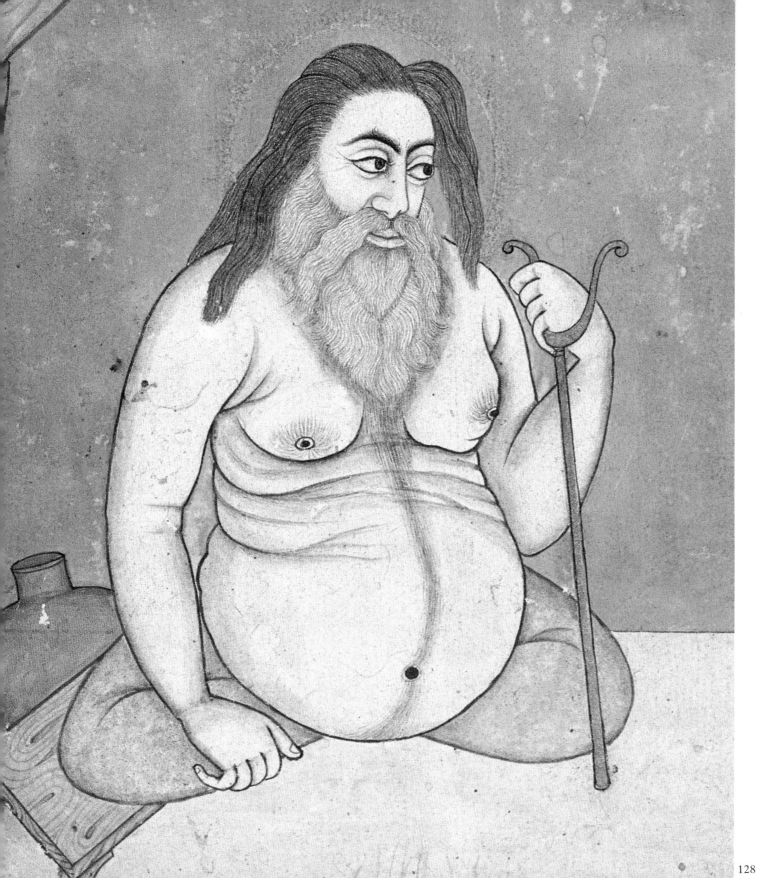

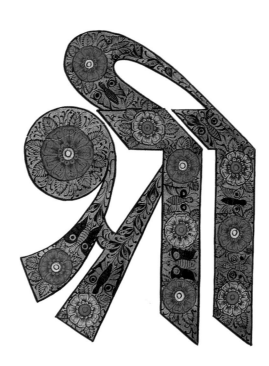

Just as a soiled mirror shines again
once it is well polished,
so does man recover his oneness
– freed from suffering, his [life's] goal achieved –
once he has seen the true nature of his self.

Shvetâshvatara Upanishad 2, 14

131

134

13

138

143

151

152

There the sun shines not, nor the moon,
nor the stars, nor these lightnings,
how much less this fire . . .
He alone shines
and everything shines in his wake.
This whole universe
shines with his light.

Shvetâshvatara Upanishad 6, 14

154

156

162

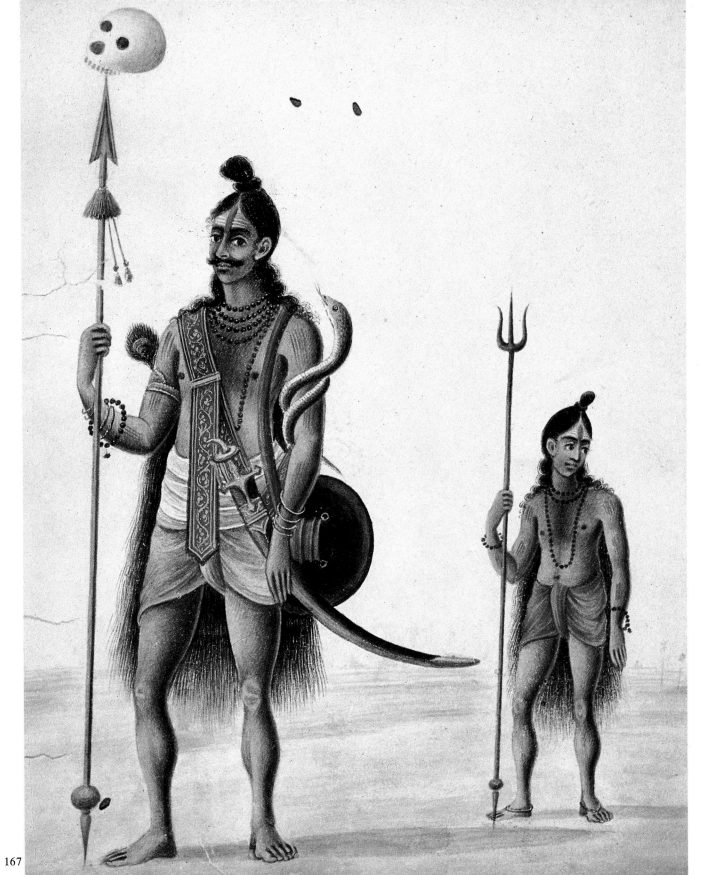

167

170

173

174

Notes on the Plates

The endpapers show two peacocks, embroidered in mirror image on a 19th-century *punkah* or fan that hangs from the ceiling of a pavilion set on a terrace in the Junagarh (Old Fort) at Bikaner, Rajasthan. In this exquisitely decorated pleasure pavilion, built in the 18th century, the ruler could recline on a couch, cooled by the breeze from this great ceiling fan – worked by a servant conveniently placed, to ensure privacy, at a lower level outside.

1 Modern folk painting on cloth of the Lord Ganesha. Hyderabad, Deccan, September 1982.

Ganesha or Ganapati, the son of the god Shiva and his wife Parvati, is the most popular of all the Hindu gods. He is chubby and elephant-headed, traditionally coloured red, and his vehicle is a mouse. No undertaking, whether religious or secular, is embarked on until Ganesha has received due honour and adoration. He is known as 'the remover of obstacles'. As the scribe responsible for copying out the Hindu sacred texts, he is the patron of writing.

In metaphysical terms, the half-human, half-elephant form of Ganesha is the classic illustration of the Indian philosophical concept of *Tat-twam-asi*, 'thou art that', in the *Chandogya Upanishad*: 'thou, an individual of seemingly circumscribed powers, art in essence cosmic truth, the Absolute.' The elephant head represents the cosmic element, the human body the individual person. Thus combined, they are one.

2 The Palace of the Winds, Jaipur, Rajasthan. Miniature, 18th century. Sackler Museum, Harvard University, Cambridge, Mass.

3 The Palace of the Winds, Jaipur, February 1985.

The Hawa Mahal (Palace of the Winds) is the most famous building in Jaipur, the Pink City. Built in 1799 during the reign of Sawai Pratap Singh, it is in fact just a vast wall pierced by 953 windows filled with filigree stone screens (*jalis*), from which the maharaja's wives and their attendants could look down on life in the bustling street below – the Sireh Deorhi Bazaar, one of the busiest thoroughfares of the town – without being seen. With its five storeys of pink sandstone, it looks like a stage set for an oriental romance. The name refers to the delicacy of the construction itself, to its openness, which allows the air to circulate freely, and – according to patronizing men – to the constant inconsequential chatter of the women within. In this picture the building is seen from the back.

4 Heroine in a pensive mood. Detail of a miniature, Pahari, Basohli, 1720. Kasturbhai Lalbhai Collection, Ahmedabad.

The miniature illustrates the *Rasamanjari*, or 'Garland of Savours', a celebrated text by the 15th-century poet Bhanudatta, which describes different types of *nayikas* or heroines and of amorous situations: the lady in the present image, we are told, is relatively inexperienced, and is longing for her lover's arrival.

5 Girl at a window. Kanota, Rajasthan, July 1987.

The naïve girl whose husband is completely devoted to her cannot believe her good fortune, and never ceases to wonder what it is about herself that inspires his devotion. 'My waist does not seem to me to be especially narrow; my breasts are not yet full; my body exudes no special radiance; my hips are not generously wide; I do not move in an easy and seductive way; my eyes do not sparkle; I am not a gifted performer of the dances that I have been taught; I am not very witty, and my laugh is not especially gay. Why is it then, O Sakhi, that he has eyes for no-one but me?'

6 Sleeping guards. Kishangarh, Rajasthan, December 1983.

One afternoon in winter, as we strolled through the courtyards of the fort at Kishangarh, we came across this telling scene of two guards who, instead of keeping watch by one of the doors, had stretched out and gone to sleep. I might have taken advantage of their sleep to penetrate further into the palace: instead I chose to record the scene – not knowing that a few years later we would come across miniatures illustrating sleeping guards in an episode from the story of Krishna.

7 Guards asleep. Detail of a miniature, Pahari, Basohli, *c.* 1755-57. Bhuri Singh Museum, Chamba, Himachal Pradesh.

The power of Maya opened the doors of the prison where Vasudeva was held, put the guards to sleep, and allowed him to escape and cross the River Yamuna, whose waters parted so that he could carry the divine infant Krishna to the other bank and on to Gokul.

8 Girls at a window. Palace of Samod, Rajasthan, July 1987.

Muslim women were never allowed out into the street without their faces being hidden by a veil, and spent most of their lives in seclusion in their private quarters. Gradually this custom of *purdah* spread to the upper ranks of Hindu society in certain regions of India, including Rajasthan. In both Urdu (the language of the Muslims) and Hindi the word *purdah* means 'curtain' or 'veil' – the veil behind which women were concealed from any man who was not a member of their immediate family. From that, it came to mean the whole system designed to protect a woman from inquiring glances and from male desire.

Purdah is regarded not as restrictive or repressive but as a sign of respectability and of social esteem. And while a woman is protected from the gaze of a hostile world, nothing prevents her from looking out at it; indeed, it appears that everything possible has been done to make that easy for her. Still today, Indian Muslim women and many of their Hindu sisters contemplate life at leisure through openwork screens (*jalis*) of wood, marble or stone, or, more often, of fine reeds, as here.

9 Women behind a reed curtain. Detail of a miniature, Pahari, Guler, 1770. Bhuri Singh Museum, Chamba, Himachal Pradesh.

10 Procession of caparisoned elephants. Detail of a miniature, Rajasthani, Jodhpur, 1825. Kumar Sangram Singh Collection, Jaipur.

11 Procession of elephants during the Teeg festival, at the City Palace, Jaipur, July 1987.

Teeg is an important festival in Rajasthan which celebrates the arrival of the monsoon, bringing the promise of cooler weather. It is held in honour of the goddess Parvati who, to mark her joy at being reunited with her husband Shiva after a long separation, promised to reward all who called upon her on this day. A statue of the goddess is placed in a palanquin and carried through the town in a procession led by camels and by painted and caparisoned elephants.

12 A snake charmer. Detail of a miniature, Rajasthani, Bundi, 1760. Prince of Wales Museum, Bombay.

The complete miniature represents the musical mode known as Asavari Ragini, after the Asavaras, an ancient jungle-dwelling tribe famous for their skill in handling snakes.

When a painter composes a *ragamala* series, he aims to convey visually the many feelings evoked by the musical modes (*ragas* and *raginis*).

13 A snake charmer. Umarkot, Sind, Pakistan, September 1981.

The snake charmer is not just an entertainer invented for the delight of tourists. His serious role emerges when a cobra has got into a house. With the help of his *murli* or flute he lures the snake out of its hiding place and then catches it in a pot or basket; there the creature is kept without food until it is safe to draw its poison fangs. Then it can be made to dance before an audience.

14 A jester playing the *sarangi*. Miniature, Mughal, 18th century, from the Large Clive Album. Victoria and Albert Museum, London.

15 *Sarangi* player. Hans Bhawan Palace, Jodhpur, Rajasthan, March 1985.

The *sarangi* is the chief bowed instrument of India: the short curved bow plays over three or four strings made of gut, below which a further thirteen metal strings serve as resonators. There are several types of *sarangi*. All are prized for their sound and for their expressive quality, and serve mainly as an accompaniment to song.

Our photograph was taken during Holi, the great spring festival of India – a time of riot and orgy whose origins are lost in the mists of time. Caste barriers are forgotten; people spray one another with coloured liquid or powder, and everyone gives free rein to fantasy and impulse. This *sarangi* player joins wholeheartedly in the universal joy.

16 Scene of village life. Kishangarh, Rajasthan, December 1983.

In India, women continue to breast-feed their children much longer than is the custom in the West. Here a two-year-old boy is being nursed by his mother, who has adjusted her *choli*, or bolero-like blouse, so that both her breasts are exposed. At the same time, she carries on with what she is doing – gathering chilli peppers that have been drying in the sun.

Chilli peppers, the dried fruit of the plant *Capsicum annum*, are a vital ingredient in Indian cookery, and are grown all over the country. After the harvest, great

scarlet carpets of chillies are spread out to dry. When they are thoroughly dried, they are pounded in a mortar or crushed and then used as a flavouring, either on their own or combined with other herbs and spices to produce the famous *masala* which is the basis for all Indian 'curry' sauces. Chilli is a fiery spice, but used with discretion it enriches the flavour of food. India is the land of spices, which for thousands of years have been prized for their medicinal and other virtues. The most popular of all, however, the famous chilli pepper, is not native: it was introduced to India from the New World at a relatively late date, probably by the Portuguese.

17 A woman nursing her child. Miniature, Rajasthani, Udaipur, 17th century. Trivandrum Museum, Kerala.

18 The little prince. Detail of a miniature, Deccani, Golconda, *c.* 1670-80. Fondation Custodia, Collection Frits Lugt, Institut Néerlandais, Paris.

The identity of this little haloed prince holding a pomegranate is unknown.

19 My friend Moon. Udaipur, Rajasthan, November 1989.

Every Indian child, whether the home he is born into is rich or poor, is adored as though he were the infant Krishna himself. He will not cry long before someone comes to comfort him. It is extremely rare to see a mother strike her child. The birth of a son is regarded as a particular blessing. In an Indian family the boy is king; in the largely female world of the home, his sisters learn to show respect to him and to wait on him as they will one day wait on their husbands.

Hemandu – 'Moon' – is for me the archetypal Hindu child.

20 The infant Krishna. Miniature, 18th century. Sackler Museum, Harvard University, Cambridge, Mass.

According to the legend, the sage Markandeya saw the Creator on the Primordial Sea in the form of an infant lying on the leaf of a banyan tree (*Ficus bengalensis*), symbol of the Cosmos. This particular manifestation represents God in profound meditation on the Ocean of Chaos, an aeon before the destruction of the universe. It signifies that dissolution is the infant stage, not the end, of the Cosmos. When Markandeya asks him who he is, he replies that he is both the Lord of the Universe, ruler, creator and destroyer of all things, and

the cosmic magician, *Maya* – illusion – who prevents men from seeing the world as it really is.

21 Rajput with a rosary. Company painting, Jaipur, *c.* 1850. Kumar Sangram Singh Collection, Jaipur.

22 Portrait of a Rajput. Udaipur bazaar, April 1982.

That the Rajput beard is still a living tradition is proved by this photograph of Shri Mohan Singh Jain. His beard perfectly fits the poet's description: 'fiercely parted down the middle into two ravening crows' wings'.

23 A scribe. Miniature attributed to Bichitr, Mughal, 1625. Knellington Collection, Harvard University Art Museum, Cambridge, Mass.

24 A scribe. City Palace, Udaipur, Rajasthan, March 1989.

The scribe or public letter-writer has played an important role in what is essentially an oral culture, for only he could record official documents and acts in a definitive form on paper. The introduction of printing and the spread of literacy have somewhat altered his function, but a scribe will always be found near a government office, ready to offer his services to villagers who have come to transact business in town.

Among the gods, it is Ganesha who is the scribe. According to tradition, when the sage Vyasa wanted someone to copy down his epic *Mahabharata* Ganesha came forward, and, it is said, wrote faster than Vyasa could dictate.

25 Rajput architecture in Udaipur. Detail of a miniature, Rajasthani, Mewar, late 18th century. National Museum, Delhi.

From their Muslim neighbours, the Mughals, the Hindu Rajputs learned a distinctive art of living that is expressed both in the refined decoration of their buildings and in their love of gardens and of running water. Outside, palaces display screened openings, balconies resting on richly carved brackets, and arcaded galleries topped by *chhatris* (little pavilions consisting of columns supporting a dome) which stand like turrets on the roofs. Inside, we find the coolness of marble, light refracted through stained glass windows, and shaped pieces of mirror darting a thousand sparks.

26 The Amet Haveli, Udaipur, December 1987.

At Udaipur, a gracious and exquisite city of dazzling

whiteness, the blue water reflects a myriad of *chhattris* like this one, photographed in the thin and pellucid air of winter.

27 Peacocks on a terrace. Detail of a miniature, Rajasthani, Kotah, *c.* 1800. State Museum, Lucknow.

The miniature, from a *Ragamala* series, depicts Setmalar Ragini, the musical mode associated with the rainy season; a female ascetic is seated in a pavilion telling her rosary, while outside on the terrace peacocks and other birds rejoice at the coming of the rain, and plants burst into lush growth.

28 A peacock spreading its tail. Jarkhand Temple, Jaipur, July 1987.

The Indian peacock, *Pavo cristatus*, is a symbol of beauty and dignity throughout Asia, but India has made it her national emblem, and here one comes across peacocks in the wild, in gardens, on terraces, and even in city streets.
    The peacock is a particularly sacred bird: in Hindu mythology it is the vehicle of Saraswati, the goddess of knowledge, and Buddhists believe that in one of his previous incarnations the Buddha was a peacock. That is why in temples little feather-dusters made of peacock plumes (which the bird sheds every year) are used to dust and to fan the thousand deities of the Hindu pantheon.

29 Peacocks on a terrace. Jarkhand Temple, Jaipur, July 1987.

From daybreak onwards, the jungle resounds to the peacock's piercing cry. To Indians, the bird seems to be saying 'Minh-ao' – 'It is going to rain'. As soon as the first raindrops fall, every peacock flies up into a tree, not to shelter from the storm but to get beyond the reach of predatory animals, who use the sound of rain as a cover to creep up on their prey. Seasoned hunters in Asia say that 'where there are peacocks there are tigers', and it seems that tigers are particularly fond of this handsome bird. The cry of the peacock, like that of the monkey, is an alarm signal telling other animals in the jungle that a predator is on the prowl.
    During the monsoon, when lightning rends the sky and thunder roars, the peacock spreads his tail and dances to attract a mate. His dance is symbolic of the re-awakening of nature, just as he himself is a symbol of fertility.

30 A peacock flying across a stormy sky. Detail

of a miniature, Rajasthani, Bundi, 1725. Museum of Fine Arts, Boston.

The miniature is one of sixteen in a *Ragamala* series.

31 Radha returns from gathering lotus flowers. Detail of a miniature, Rajasthani, Bundi, 18th century. Prince of Wales Museum, Bombay.

The complete miniature shows Krishna looking out of a palace window to admire Radha and other *gopis* (milkmaids) who have been gathering white lotus flowers in a pool.

32 Sahira, a girl with a waterlily. Hyderabad, Deccan, September 1982.

This girl holding a waterlily that she has just picked from a pool irresistibly suggests the *nayika* or heroine that Indian typology describes as 'the innocent girl who does not suspect the onset of adolescence'. This is how the poet Bhanudatta (see caption 4) describes her: 'Adolescence has taken her by surprise. The *nayika* whose face resembles the moon is standing beside a pool, drying herself. Her gleaming eyes, of which the water sends back reflections, are like lotus flowers. She thinks that flower buds may still be hanging, tangled, from her ears, and waves her hands to brush them away. She then looks down at her body, which is covered with a silky down; taking this for seaweed, she tries to rub it off. Her hips have become fuller. In her virginal innocence, she keeps asking her companion, "Am I weary? What is the matter with me?"'

33 A woman holding two lotus flowers. Detail of a miniature, Rajasthani, Kishangarh, 18th century. Private Collection.

34 Chumki (woman with a lotus). Hyderabad, Deccan, September 1982.

Vatsyayana's famous treatise on sexual love, the *Kama Sutra*, divides Indian women into four main types, of which the most desirable is the *padmini*, the lotus-woman: 'The Padmini has the following physical and moral qualities: her face is comely as the full moon; her rounded body is soft as mustard flower [*shira*]; her skin is delicate, tender and pale as the yellow lotus, never dark; her eyes are lovely and brilliant as those of a doe, well defined, with a dot of red at the corner; her breasts are firm, full, and high; her neck is well defined, her nose straight and clearly drawn; there are three folds or wrinkles on her belly around her navel; her vagina [*yoni*] is like a half-open

lotus bud, and her love-fluid [*kamasalila*] has the scent of a lily before it has come into full bloom. She moves like a swan, and her low, musical voice is like that of the cuckoo [*kokila*]. She likes new clothes, precious jewels, and rich fabrics. She eats little, sleeps lightly, and, being as respectful and pious as she is intelligent and courteous, takes pleasure in worshipping the gods and in listening to the conversation of Brahmins.'

35 Lotus in a pool. Shrawantal, Kanha wildlife sanctuary, Madhya Pradesh, June 1978.

36 A couple making love on a bed of water plants. Erotic miniature, Rajasthani, Sirohi, *c.* 1800. Kumar Sangram Singh Collection, Jaipur.

Chapter IX of the *Kama Sutra* is entitled 'Of the woman who plays the part of the man'. Here we read: 'When a woman sees that her lover is tired by a protracted congress before her own desires are gratified, she should, with his permission, turn him on to his back and assist him by taking his place. She may also act thus to satisfy the curiosity of her lover or her own wish for novelty.' One verse says specifically: 'Even if a woman is reserved and conceals her feelings, in mounting the man she displays to him all her love and all her desire.'

37 Devi, the Great Goddess. Detail of a miniature, Pahari, Basohli, 1660-70. Brooklyn Museum, New York.

Devi is the Great Goddess, the Resplendent One, the female principle, the *shakti* or immanent energy, which in Hindu mythology is always represented as a female deity, the consort of the male deity. Devi is the combined power of Shiva, Vishnu and Brahma. For her devotees, the Shaktas, the source of life seen as female is the supreme manifestation of the divine. God is a woman.
    The eternal couple, Shiva and Shakti, represented by male and female emblems, the *lingam* and the *yoni*, remain at the heart of Hinduism today. The phallus embraced by the vulva is the central object of devotion. The widespread cult of the mother figure is chiefly focused on Parvati, the consort of Shiva.
    This miniature showing Devi drinking a bowl of wine comes from a set of Tantric representations of the Great Goddess.
    Basohli painting is characterized by the liberal use of fragments of beetle wings that glitter like emeralds.

38 Maharana Fateh Singh of Mewar. Detail of

a miniature, Rajasthani, Mewar, 19th century. Shiv Niwas Palace, Udaipur, Rajasthan.

Fateh Singh, known as 'the Light of the Hindus', is regarded by many as the last true Indian ruler.

39 Shri Arvind Singh Mewar, Maharana of Udaipur, posing in state dress in his palace, December 1987.

Mewar's place at the head of all the Rajput clans was well deserved: alone among Hindu princes, its rulers never intermarried with the Mughals. After eight hundred years of almost ceaseless struggle against the Muslim invaders, the Mewaris managed to retain the same territory that they had themselves conquered a thousand years earlier.

40 A Mughal princess. Miniature on ivory, late Mughal, 1835. Krishna Riboud Collection, Paris.

She is the favourite daughter of Akbar Shah II, who reigned in Delhi 1806-37, and her portrait is the work of Muhammad Azim Azul.

41 Portrait of Aruna. Bombay, July 1977.

In the words of Bhanudatta, 'Her high birth prevents her from expressing herself in any way but through the barely discernible movement of her pupils; a smile hovers over her lower lip. When she speaks, her voice is so soft that her words are heard only by the beloved.'

42 A royal princess seated under a tent-like baldacchino. Detail of a miniature, Mughal, 18th century. Lahore Museum, Pakistan.

43 A pavilion in the fort at Lahore, Pakistan, April 1971.

This little pavilion in the Shish Mahal (Mirror Palace) courtyard, with its curious curved roof, is a royal tent realized in marble in 1631. It is known as Naulakha (900,000) because it cost 900,000 rupees: it contains the finest examples in all Lahore of *pietra dura* work, in which cunningly wrought pieces of semi-precious stone are set into marble panels to form geometric or floral patterns.

44 Two female lovers. Detail of a miniature, Mughal, 18th century. Bharat Kala Bhavan, Varanasi.

Although traditionally women have occupied a position of some importance in Indian society, it is not surprising that in a country where Muslim influence has been felt for centuries there is a profound sense of the gulf separating the sexes. The atmosphere of the *zenana* – the women's quarters, like the *harem* – has not entirely disappeared and some women in the upper ranks of society still lead a fairly frivolous and idle life. Within the *zenana*, against a backdrop of intrigues and power struggles between the women, close friendships also sprang up, giving rise to the theme of female lovers which is often found in miniatures.

45 Tenderness. Udaipur, December 1987.

46 A woman adjusting her *dupatta* (veil). Detail of a miniature, Mughal, 18th century. Reza Library, Rampur, Uttar Pradesh.

47 A Muslim bride. Rampur, January 1984.

Muslim law permits a man to have up to four wives, so long as he has the means to support them and can treat them all fairly. A proverb attributed to the Mughals says: 'A man should marry four wives – a Persian, to have someone with whom he can converse; a woman from Khurasan, to run the household; a Hindu, to look after his children; and a woman from Mavarunnahr, to beat as a warning to the other three.'

48 A woman consumed by the fever of love. Detail of a miniature, Rajasthani, Bundi, 18th century. Bharat Kala Bhavan, Varanasi.

Passion rages in the body of this young woman, stretched out on luxurious cushions. She is burning with love, but her lover is absent, and nothing can soothe her fever – not the gentle breeze that blows from the garden, cooled by fountains in a pool where lotus bloom, nor the rosewater with which a servant sprinkles her body, nor the fruits and lotions on the ground beside her couch.

49 Reshma. Palace of Samod, Rajasthan, July 1987.

We see here a *mugdha nayika*, an inexperienced girl, 'beginning to be aware of [her] body's blossoming'.

When King Kama, the god of love, set up his dwelling in the body of a *mughda*, he began to reconstruct it with care. Under his direction her eye became as playful as that of a wagtail, her face took on the roundness of the full moon, and her voice assumed the soursweet tone of the waves in a sea of nectar.

50 A miniaturist at work in the studio of Kumar Sangram Singh, Jaipur, March 1982.

We have been privileged to learn about the art of miniature painting not only through museums but through the expert guidance of remarkable private collectors. Some, among them Shri Mohan Lal Gupta, patiently taught us to distinguish between the many schools of Rajasthani painting.

Prince Kumar Sangram Singh has revived an ancestral tradition by setting up a studio in Jaipur where some dozen miniaturists work, drawing inspiration from the best pictures in his collection. They are copyists; but they work in an age-old tradition, and come as close as possible to the spirit and technique of the original paintings, using the same hand-made rag paper, the same pigments (mostly mineral in origin), and the same squirrel-hair brushes. What saddened us was to see the cheerless setting in which these miniaturists worked, and the drab European clothes that they wore. Kumar Sangram Singh understood our dismay, and from trunks he produced a whole array of things to brighten up the painters. Quickly and decisively, helped by his son Surya Vijay Singh and the latter's wife, Brigitte, the workshop was transformed before our eyes into a scene worthy of the magnificence of a Mughal emperor or a princely patron.

In Jaipur there are several hundred miniaturists at work today; among them are a few genuinely talented artists, such as the famous Bannu, who not only copies and restores earlier miniatures but is capable of original creation.

51 Modern copy of a self-portrait of the miniaturist Sahib Ram (Rajasthani, Jaipur, 1780). Kumar Sangram Singh Collection, Jaipur.

52 A display of moustaches. Miniature, Pahari, 19th century. Bharat Kala Bhavan, Varanasi.

These two men preening their moustaches look as though each is using the other as a mirror.

53 Rajput moustaches. Udaipur, Rajasthan, November 1989.

In Rajasthan men are as vain as women, and villagers are no less proud of their appearance than princes. They are not self-conscious about wearing gold jewelry – rings, necklaces, or earrings – and they wear it with such dignity that no-one could possibly consider them effeminate. However, with the exception of the turban, the part of a Rajput's appearance of which he takes the greatest care and in which he takes the greatest pride is his moustache, which is always immaculately sleek and sometimes curled up at the tips.

Devi Singh is posing here next to a full-length portrait of Maharana Sajjan Singh (ruled 1874-84) in the Sajjan Singh Niwas, a suite in the famous Lake Palace Hotel, on an island in Lake Pichola.

54 A raja smoking a *huqqa* (water-pipe) and gazing at himself in a mirror. Wall-painting, City Palace, Udaipur, 19th century.

There are two kinds of wall-painting in Rajasthan. The humbler kind are used on the occasion of a wedding to decorate door-surrounds and the exterior walls of houses, where they will remain until the next wedding takes place. Their subject-matter is usually the most popular gods, or else warriors, horsemen or elephants. The other kind of mural, which adorns the inner walls of rooms, pavilions and halls in palaces or in *havelis* (patrician houses), takes its style from miniature painting.

Each princely state developed its own manner: that of Mewar, which emerged in the 15th century, is characterized by bright colours and vigorous draughtsmanship, qualities that are displayed in this wall-painting in the Chitram ki Burj, a charming pavilion in the City Palace, where a servant girl appears to be holding a mirror for Maharana Jawan Singh (ruled 1828-38).

55 In the following painting, we see the same prince smoking a *huqqa*, together with his reflection in the mirror.

56 Princes playing chess. Miniature, Pahari, Kangra, 18th century. Bharat Kala Bhavan, Varanasi.

57 Nawab Mir Abdullah playing chess with his son Jafar. Lucknow, September 1987.

The game of chess is believed to have originated in India. It is said to have been invented by Shesha, the prime minister of King Shriram, to demonstrate to the ruler's dissolute son that a ruler without the support of his people is doomed. Shriram was so delighted with the new game that he had chessboards set up in all the temples. He then called on Shesha to name his reward. The prime minister asked that a single grain of rice be put in the first square of the chessboard, that the number should be doubled in the second, doubled again in the third, and so on until the end, and that he then be given the total number of grains. The king protested that this was far too modest a reward, but Shesha was adamant, and Shriram gave orders that his request should be carried out.

When the royal treasurer had calculated the requisite number of grains, he came trembling before his lord and said that the command was impossible to execute: while there would only be one grain in the first square, two in the second, and four in the third, the sixteenth square called for 32,768 grains – the equivalent of a pound of wheat – and the fortieth would require the stock of 1,024 stores. By the time the sixty-fourth square was reached, the necessary quantity could be obtained only by requisitioning the complete contents of all the granaries in 16,384 towns. Since there were not that many towns in the whole of the kingdom, the order could not be obeyed. The ruler was delighted by this demonstration of Shesha's wisdom, and granted him many rich gifts, saying that the ingenuity he had demonstrated in formulating his request was even greater than the talent required to invent the game in the first place.

58 A Mughal lady. Miniature, Mughal, late 16th century. Musée Guimet, Paris.

We were particularly intrigued by the ring that this elegant lady is wearing on her right hand, in which she appears to be gazing at her reflection.

59 Begum Sahiba. Tonk, Rajasthan, March 1989.

We found an identical mirror ring worn by Begum Sahiba, the widow of His Highness Nawab Mohammad Ismail Ali Khan Sahib, the last ruler of the tiny Muslim state of Tonk in Rajasthan, who died in 1979. The mirror ring, she told us, is used by a bride on the day of her wedding to glimpse for the first time the face of her husband-to-be.

On the ground in front of Begum Sahiba is a silver box containing *pan*, or betel leaf, which is a popular refreshment throughout all the regions and social classes of India. The rules of hospitality demand that *pan* be offered to guests at the end of any meal. Ordinary *pan* contains, in addition to the betel leaf, only a little slaked lime mixed with water and areca nut, but when it is flavoured with scented coconut, cardamon, cloves, aniseed and saffron, it becomes a substance for refined palates. *Pan* is considered to be an excellent aid to digestion, and to freshen the breath. Like cigarettes in the West, however, it can become addictive: some people chew *pan* up to a hundred times a day.

60 The syllable *om*. Miniature, Pahari, Kangra, 18th century. Bharat Kala Bhavan, Varanasi.

As depicted here, it contains the three great gods of

the Hindu *trimurti* – Brahma (with four heads), Vishnu (coloured dark blue and seated on a lotus), and Shiva (with his trident and crescent moon headdress) – and two other figures.

Om is regarded as the most sacred of all utterances. It represents the primordial sound, and in itself comprehends all other sounds. It is the most abstract symbol of the divine, and the means of mystical enlightenment. It is both self-denial and self-realization. As a monosyllabic *mantra* – a formula for invoking the divine – it is also known as 'the ferryman', because it conveys man to the other shore, to an awareness of the divine, release from earthly bonds, and perception of the ultimate Reality.

61 Astronomers carrying out observations. Miniature, Mughal, 1840, from a Sanskrit treatise on astrology. British Library, London.

62 A *pandit* at work in the Observatory, Jaipur, 2 March 1985.

This is the finest and best preserved of the five observatories built in various parts of India by Maharaja Jai Singh II (1699-1743), creator of the city of Jaipur, capital of Rajasthan, whose name has gone down in history as a politician, town-planner and astronomer. The Jantar Mantar in Jaipur, built of stone and marble in one of the courtyards of the palace, is fascinating both architecturally and technically. Not least remarkable is the fact that its many instruments are still used today by *pandits* (sages and scholars) to carry out observations to determine the most auspicious dates for the celebration of important religious festivals.

The two circular rings seen here are made of an alloy of seven metals and held between stone pillars. Each circle, divided into 360 degrees, turns on an axis that is parallel to the rotational axis of the earth. Holding a hollow tube against the edge, the *pandit* looks up at the sky, and from the position of a heavenly body in relation to the calibrated rim calculates its position in space.

63 An Indian bull. Glass-painting, Juna Mahal (Old Palace), Duṅgarpur, Rajasthan, 19th century.

64 Purnima (Full Moon), an Indian cow. Mataji Santosh ashram, Saurashtra, November 1987.

65 Milking at Nathdwara, Rajasthan, December 1987.

Nothing is more sacred than the milk of cows, the

animals who figure largely in the life of Krishna, the most celebrated *avatar* of Vishnu. Hindus believe that when you eat anything you absorb its specific qualities: cow's milk is thus preferable to water-buffalo milk, for the latter would make you heavy and lazy like the water-buffalo itself. Krishna grew up among cows in an idyllic pastoral world, and his paradise, Goloka, is the dwelling-place of Surabhi, the cow who answers all prayers on Mount Meru.

Each part of the cow, from her nostrils to the tip of her tail, is the home of a specific deity. The cult of the sacred cow spread in Brahmanical times, and to kill a cow became as serious an offence as to kill a Brahmin.

66 A cowherd milking his cow, who turns to lick her calf. Detail of a relief in the Cave of Krishna, one of the Pandava Caves at Mamallapuram, south of Madras, early 7th century.

The complete relief shows Krishna holding up Mount Govardhan to shelter cows from a terrible storm provoked by the jealousy of Indra.

67 Churning butter. Detail of a miniature, Rajasthani, Jodhpur, 18th century. Alwar Museum, Rajasthan.

The churning of butter is traditionally associated with the myth of the creation of the world, when the gods and demons churned the primordial Ocean of Milk.

Indra, king of the gods, had been stripped of all his possessions by demons. The Lord Vishnu advised him to seek reconciliation with the latter and to enlist their help in churning the Ocean of Milk to produce ambrosia (*amrita*), which would make the gods immortal and restore their lost power. So the gods and demons set about churning the Ocean. The first product of this joint venture is a deadly poison, *halahala*: Shiva, the beneficent, swallows it, thus saving the worlds from certain destruction. Next there emerges a cow, then a white horse, an elephant, the matchless jewel, the tree that grants all wishes, the goddess of fortune, the goddess of wine, and the doctor of the gods. Each takes what he can; but the demons, breaking the original agreement whereby the *amrita* was to be divided equally between the two groups, seize the vase containing the elixir of immortality. Vishnu then disguises himself as the enchantress Mohini, gains possession of the vase, and cleverly arranges to divide its contents only among the gods, who regain their strength, fall upon the demons, and recover their lost sovereignty.

68 Village scene. Rajasthan, November 1989.

Two women are churning butter, using one of the oldest technological inventions in the world: a stick fitted with blades is made to turn in a pot by means of a rope wound round its shank which the women pull alternately with an even motion, often accompanying themselves by stories spoken or sung.

69 Women carrying water. Detail of a miniature, Pahari, Kangra, 18th century. Bharat Kala Bhavan, Varanasi.

India is a predominantly rural country, and most houses have no running water. Fetching water is a woman's chief task: morning and evening, day after day, she sets off with a pot made of earthenware or brass which she will balance on her head and carry back, filled with the precious, indispensable liquid. Alone, or more often with other women from her village, she goes down to the river, to the village watering place – often just a stagnant pool fed by infrequent rains and used also by livestock – or to a communal well. Many miniatures depict the story of a woman giving water to a prince, who invariably falls in love with her.

70 Women returning from fetching water. South bank of the Narmada River, Omkareshwar, Madhya Pradesh, January 1990.

At the source of water the women meet, gossip and giggle, in gatherings that are some compensation for the drudgery of the task. Women returning from the river present a magnificent silhouette: the weight of the vessels on their heads gives their walk a majestic elegance and sway.

71 Preparing and cooking *chapatis* in a Rajasthani village, November 1987.

There are no bakers in the Indian subcontinent. Bread is specially prepared before every meal in each individual house and local inn. Every morning, the amount of wheat needed for the day's baking is ground in a little stone quern. Only when everyone is ready to eat does the housewife roll out the unleavened dough on a small wooden board and cook the thin patties on a very slightly curved iron surface. The *chapatis* are served hot as an accompaniment to dishes of spiced vegetables.

72 Women preparing *chapatis*. Detail of a miniature, Pahari, Kangra, 18th century. Bharat Kala Bhavan, Varanasi.

The complete miniature shows Brahmins performing

puja (making an offering) in the courtyard of a house while women carry out various domestic duties.

73 Dilkash with her parrot. Hyderabad, Deccan, January 1984.

The parrot, *tota*, is the most common pet in Indian households. Classic literature and poetry have made much of a creature whose gift of speech suits it to be the witness, confidant, friend and protector of lovers. In one story, a lover setting out on a journey teaches his parrot endearments to repeat to his beloved during his absence. A young woman holding a parrot in a cage or with a parrot perched on her shoulder is a popular subject in both sculpture and miniature painting. In the famous 12th-century *Tuti-nama*, or 'Tale of a Parrot', a parrot who is a veritable Sheherezade keeps his mistress amused night after night with enthralling tales of adultery to keep her from joining her lover while her husband is away.

It is no coincidence that the parrot is the vehicle of Kama, the god of love.

74 A young woman with her parrot. Miniature, Deccani, 18th century. Salar Jang Museum, Hyderabad.

75 Portrait of a woman. Detail of a miniature, Rajasthani, Jaipur, *c.* 1750. Kumar Sangram Singh Collection, Jaipur.

76 Portrait of Renuka. Ahmedabad, October 1982.

Certain physical types recur over the centuries, or so it seems. For me, the features of the girl I photographed in a mirror had an uncanny resemblance to those of the girl in the miniature, above all the size of the eyes – enormous eyes, like those which an Indian poet described as 'whispering to her ears', meaning that they were so large that they seemed to take up her whole face from ear to ear.

77 A lotus flower made of semi-precious stones inlaid in marble. Detail of modern *pietra dura* work on the Samadhi, a funerary monument under construction at Dayalbagh on the outskirts of Agra.

The monument to Soamiji Maharaj, one of many such founders of religious sects in India, was begun in 1904, twenty-six years after his death in 1878, and is still under construction, fuelled slowly by contributions from his followers. The most optimistic assessment suggests that this gigantic mausoleum, even larger than the Taj Mahal, will not be completed until around the year 2025 – making a total of some 120 years. But in India time counts for little, and ancient craft techniques are still alive.

The lotus can be regarded as the national flower of India. Brahma sprang from a mystic lotus growing out of the navel of Vishnu. Lakshmi and countless other goddesses are often shown seated on a throne made of lotus petals. The lotus is the very image of the universe – the flower that blooms in all its glory in the bosom of the formless, infinite causal Ocean, and in the various stages of its blossoming represents worlds and beings at different stages in their evolutionary development.

78 The Baha'i Temple, Delhi, January 1988.

That the lotus can be a source of inspiration today is proved by the new Baha'i Temple in Delhi, designed by an Iranian architect based in Canada, which is perhaps the most successful religious building of the 20th century. It is a remarkable feat of engineering which took the architect ten years to evolve: it represents a combination of age-old skills, contributed by some ten thousand Indian craftsmen, with the most advanced technology, in the form of four hundred structural drawings by a team of twelve engineers. The marble, 9,000 cubic metres of it, was quarried in Greece, shaped in Italy with the aid of a computer, shipped to India, and set up in Delhi. Two circles of lotus petals – an inner ring forming the dome, and an outer one of nine petals each containing an entrance – rise from a pool of water. The result is a masterpiece.

79 The footprints of Vishnu. Miniature, Pahari, Mankot, 18th century. Chandigarh Museum.

The footprints of Vishnu symbolize the oneness of divine Manifestation. All the elements of the universe are represented by particular signs, each a reference to a key aspect of the Ultimate. Since all things are essentially One, there can be an infinite number of fragments of the supreme Oneness, which must all be seen as individual signs of the one Reality. Vishnu's footprints are a revelation of his role as cosmic man.

According to esoteric Hindu tradition, the heel and big toe contain special channels which are second in importance only to the *nadis*, the vessels in the spinal column. Through them, primordial energy can penetrate the physical body.

80 The Emperor Babur crossing the Son River on a bridge of boats. Miniature from a *Baburnama* (Story of Babur), Mughal, 16th century. National Museum, New Delhi.

Babur (1483-1530), founder of the Mughal Empire in India, left behind him remarkable memoirs which are a classic of world literature. The miniature illustrates the following passage from his account: 'On Thursday [14 April 1529] we left the camp by boat. All the boats that had assembled were ordered to set out as soon as I arrived and to link themselves together so as to form a single line. That line was much longer than the river was wide, even though not all the boats had come together. It was impossible to advance in this way for long, because the river varied in depth and strength of current from one place to another. In the midst of the boats a gavial [Indian crocodile] appeared. This frightened a fish, which leapt into the air so high that it fell back into one of the boats. It was picked up and brought to me...'

81 Bridge of boats over the Yamuna, Delhi, January 1984.

Bridges of boats are still used in India and Pakistan today, though they are becoming less and less common. They have to be dismantled during the monsoon, so are of use only during the dry season.

82 A man reading a scroll written in Persian. Miniature, Mughal, *c.* 1565-70. Musée Guimet, Paris.

This is in fact a portrait of the famous Persian miniaturist Mir Mosawwir of Tabriz, painted by his son, Mir Sayyid Ali, who became one of the great masters of Mughal painting in the 16th century (the Emperor Humayun said of him that he could paint on a single grain of rice a whole team of horsemen playing polo). Mir Sayyid Ali began his career in Persia at the court of Shah Tahmasp, then moved to Kabul in Afghanistan, where he set up the school of painting founded by Humayun, and finally followed that emperor to India.

83 A Hindu merchant working on his accounts. Bazaar, Ajmer, Rajasthan, March 1987.

Absorbed in his account book, which looks rather like a calendar with an impossible number of pages, this jeweller sits with his index finger cocked in what seems a gesture of utter perplexity. His turban, his steel-rimmed spectacles, his pen and inkwell, his comfortable pose suggestive of a *hatha yoga* position, the cushion on which the account book rests – every detail is redolent of an old, unchanging East which, no matter how relentlessly or aggressively it is under attack from the dynamic West, miraculously continues to live its own distinctive life.

Indians are formidable accountants: it is not an accident that they invented what we call 'arabic' numerals. Indian functionaries are meticulous to the point of mania, and this can result in scarcely imaginable quibbles. The sight, in offices, of bundles of files tied together with string and piled right up to the ceiling is amazing and appalling. And yet, within this apparent chaos, everything is indexed, classified, filed away, and located when necessary – for any self-respecting Indian clerk, like an elephant, never forgets.

84 An ear-cleaner. Gol Darwaza, Old Lucknow, September 1987.

The *kansafwallah*, or ear-cleaner, is a traditional figure on the urban scene in India. He wears a flat red turban, and can be recognized by the strands of cotton tucked behind his own ear, in much the same way as a bookkeeper temporarily parks his pencil or pen. His equipment consists of a tiny silver spoon with which he extracts the wax, tufts of cotton used to cleanse the eardrum, and warm mustard oil, and his consulting room is the street itself, where he and his client squat unselfconsciously.

85 An ear-cleaner. Company painting from the Skinner Album, 1825. British Library, London.

86 An entertainer with performing monkeys and a trained goat. Company painting from the Skinner Album, 1825. British Library, London.

87 A street entertainer with his performing monkey. New Delhi, January 1988.

It is surely because they are so clever at imitating people that monkeys are among the funniest and most moving of all performing animals. Dressed in a little skirt and with bells around his paws, this one is executing a *kathak* dance to the accompaniment of a jangling tambourine played by his master. (*Kathak* is a court style of dancing which was especially popular with the Muslim rulers of India and is still performed today by many girls in upper-class homes.) Street entertainers are very popular in India, and performing monkeys collect money from their audience by hanging firmly on to the spectators' clothes until they extract from them the last possible tiny coin.

88 A fairground wheel. Miniature, Rajasthani, Jodhpur, 18th century. Kumar Sangram Singh Collection, Jaipur.

89 Fairground wheel in the Nizamuddin district of New Delhi, January 1984.

India is the land of festivals, where popular religious feeling finds its fullest expression. Large crowds flock to the pilgrimage sites, often in quite small villages, and the arrival of the crowds is an impressive sight. In a few days, or even a few hours, thousands of people converge from all directions on foot, or in carts, tractors and buses. Religious festivals are nearly always accompanied by a fair – a *mela* – and a market; a whole canvas town springs up for a day or two, offering refreshment booths, displays of sweetmeats, and the wares of countless merchants and pedlars. Street entertainers, acrobats and story-tellers keep the crowd amused; children love the fairground wheels.

The wheel in the photograph had been set up during the celebrations of the *urs* of Sheikh Nizam ud-din Aulia, the anniversary of his death (see caption 104), which had taken place six hundred years earlier in the district that contains his tomb and bears his name today.

90 A bear-leader. Miniature, Mughal, 18th century. Alwar Museum, Rajasthan.

It seems that this is in fact an allegorical image: the bear-leader represents the man of noble spirit, while the bear represents the baser instincts that he struggles to overcome. The man is depicted as a wandering dervish. The marks of burns on his body tell of the self-mortification that he has practised in his battles with unclean thoughts.

91 A bear-leader. Jaipur, July 1977.

The animal belongs to the species *Merlusus ursinus*, the playful, acrobatic animals known throughout northern India as *bhalu*. Bears that are to be trained are usually taken away from their mothers as very young cubs and bottle-fed by their trainers; when they are a year old their teeth are pulled out and a ring is inserted in their sensitive nose, to which a rope is attached to ensure their obedience. Fed on the wheat-flour cakes known as *chapatis*, a bear may live to serve his master for as long as thirty years.

92, 93 An itinerant photographer photographing and photographed. Hampi, Karnataka, April 1966.

From the time of its first appearance in India, around 1840, Indians have been fascinated by the camera. Maharajas ordered the best equipment from England and greeted the novelty with enthusiasm. Miniature painters gave up and turned to photography. A genre that achieved remarkable results was the painted photograph, which made use of the traditional skills and aesthetic training of professional miniaturists. Maharaja Sawai Ram Singh II of Jaipur went so far as to set up a photographic studio within the walls of his palace. It is said that the exposure times in that studio were measured not by the clock but by the recitation of mantras (sacred chants) calculated to give exactly the right result.

94 A lady drawing back her hair. Detail of a miniature, Pahari, Basohli, 1720. Kasturbhai Lalbhai Collection, Ahmedabad.

The miniature, from a *Rasamanjari*, depicts the type of *nayika* or heroine characterized by Bhanudatta as neither in a good nor in a bad mood, who abstractedly sits and draws back her long hair.

95 Shikha, at the Hanuman temple, Ahmedabad, February 1989.

Indian women are famous for the beauty and length of their hair, into which they love to rub oil and perfume.

96 A Marwari horse. Tilwara livestock fair, Rajasthan, March 1985.

97 A woman selling *pan*, against the background of a folk wall-painting showing the same breed of horse in parade harness. Dwarkadesh Temple, Kankroli, Rajasthan.

Horses of this breed, which originated at Marwar near Jodhpur, are characterized by their inward-pointing ears. The horse is the symbol of the Kshatriya or warrior caste, and it is inextricably associated with the Rajputs, who claim descent from the first Aryan invaders of India. In addition to the historic account of their origins, there is also a mythological one: according to this, most Rajput kings are descended from Surya, the Sun, whose chariot is drawn by seven horses. Rajput horsemen are celebrated, and the history of Rajputana – the modern Rajasthan – is filled with tales of chivalry and valorous exploits.

The relationship between the animal and his master was so close that the horse's trappings were as rich as his master's clothing and jewels: on his head was an aigrette like that worn by the prince, and his breast was garlanded with necklaces of gold or silver and precious stones.

98 The syllable *om*. Miniature, Sikh, *c.* 1830-40. Ranjit Singh Museum, Amritsar.

This miniature, with representations of the three chief deities of the Hindu pantheon with their consorts – Brahma and Saraswati, Vishnu and Lakshmi, and Shiva and Parvati – comes from a military instruction manual written in Persian script.

Om is the sound symbolizing the Absolute, uttered at the beginning of all sacred chants, which stands for the ultimate spiritual Reality. Transcribed as *aum*, it has three letters, corresponding to the *trimurti* (the Hindu trinity) and the three *gunas* or qualities: *a* is Brahma, the great Being, the orbiting tendency (*raja*), the colour red, and the power of action; *u* is Vishnu, the Indwelling, the cohesive tendency (*sattvas*), the colour white, and the power of knowledge; *m* is Shiva, the Lord of Sleep, the disintegrative tendency (*tamas*), the colour black, and the power of will. These are followed by a half-letter representing that which has no qualities and is perceptible only to yogis.

99 Camel-riders. Miniature, Rajasthani, Jodhpur, 18th century. Kumar Sangram Singh Collection, Jaipur.

100 A camel-rider. Pushkar fair, Rajasthan, November 1966.

Every year at the time of the full moon in the month of Kartik (October-November) a great religious festival involving ritual bathing takes place at the lake of Pushkar, near Ajmer. The festival is accompanied by a trade fair and cattle show, of which the stars are the camels (*Camelus dromedarius*), the most photogenic of all the creatures of the desert and also the best adapted and most useful. Dromedaries are a godsend in dry regions, where they carry goods, draw water from wells, provide transport, and pull ploughs. At the Pushkar fair, decorated with strings of blue beads, bells and garlands, and harnessed as if for a parade, the dromedary is king, and bets are laid on which animal can carry the heaviest load or run the fastest.

101 An old man smoking a *huqqa*. Miniature, Mughal, late 16th century. National Museum, New Delhi.

The Portuguese brought tobacco to India in the 16th century, and it was greeted with enthusiasm at Akbar's court. The *huqqa*, or water-pipe, was introduced at about the same time from Persia. At first smoking was a courtly activity, associated with luxury and relaxation (a special servant was employed to prepare his master's pipes); but soon it spread among the people, and specialized industries grew up. Craftsmen and jewellers created *huqqas* to suit all purses and all tastes – *huqqas* with long flexible tubes or short rigid ones, mouthpieces made of base metal, copper, silver, earthenware or glazed ceramic. The principle remains the same: the smoke is cooled by being drawn through water. Today *huqqas* have somewhat fallen out of fashion, but they remain popular among country people.

102 A Saurashtrian enjoying his *huqqa*, November 1987.

Earthenware is favoured by true connoisseurs as the best material for retaining the flavour and for cooling tobacco smoke.

103 A Muslim saint. Detail of a miniature, Mughal, 17th century. Reza Library, Rampur, Uttar Pradesh.

104 Sufi Baba. Ajmer *urs*, March 1987.

The tombs of saints, both Hindu and Muslim, are the subject of great popular devotion in India, and they form the centrepiece of pilgrimages that attract vast numbers of people. The most important of all is at Ajmer in Rajasthan, where the great 14th-century Muslim saint Muyyin ud-din Chishti is buried. Every year immense crowds assemble, in a mood of intense religious fervour, to commemorate with prayers, music and singing the anniversary of his death. Such an anniversary is known as *urs* – literally, 'wedding', for 'our death is our wedding to eternity'. Among the pilgrims many, like this venerable old white-bearded man, are dervishes.

105 A Muslim reading. Detail of the upper border of a Mughal miniature, 1640. Musée Guimet, Paris.

The border surrounds a portrait of a dignitary at the court of Shah Jahan.

106 Jami Masjid, Delhi, March 1971.

This photograph has the clarity, the precision and the spareness of an old print.

The great congregational mosque in Delhi is the largest in all India, and was built by Shah Jahan in 1644-58. With the linear precision of its silhouette, it is the perfect expression of Mughal classicism. The mosque, raised on a high platform and reached through three gates at the top of three great stairways, forms a haven of peace and prayer in the midst of the most bustling of all Indian bazaars. This is the heart of Muslim Old Delhi – a spiritual heart, that

beats five times a day at the call of the muezzin; but also a fairground, a theatre and a perpetual circus. Chess-players, acrobats and story-tellers compete for space with ear-cleaners, dentists, masseurs, astrologers, and wrestlers; here you will find sellers of perfumes and of every possible kind of merchandise, potion or pill, bird-markets, flea-markets – and thieves.

107 A Nihang Akali, of the strictest order among the Sikhs. Company painting from the Skinner Album, 1825. British Library, London.

108 Nihangs in conversation. Akali Phula Singh Dera Burj, Amritsar, December 1989.

Sikhism was founded in 1469 by Guru Nanak as a religious brotherhood based on a reformed Hinduism combined with some elements drawn from Islam. Among the Sikhs the Nihangs (from the Persian word for crocodile), established in 1699 by Guru Gobind, the tenth and last Sikh Guru, form an élite military corps who in the past often distinguished themselves in combat with the Afghans and the British. Even when they are not armed, which they almost always are, they can be recognized by their blue uniform and tall turban topped with steel discs. These redressers of wrongs and guardians of the Sikh faith bring to mind thoughts of ancient chivalry and heroic deeds.

109 Jain nuins. Miniature, Western India, 17th century. Private Collection

These two nuns are on their way to a temple in the mountains to honour one of the twenty-four Jain saints or Tirthankaras, 'those who lead to the other shore'.

Jainism (from the Sanskrit *jina*, conqueror, in the sense of one who has conquered earthly passions) was founded in India in the 6th century BC by a sage known as Mahavira, the Great Hero. Its basic tenet is *ahimsa*, non-violence; Jains are prohibited from killing or mistreating all creatures, even the most seemingly insignificant. Their diet is correspondingly restricted: they eat only fruit and vegetables, and drink only filtered water. Among some four millions Jains in India today there are many monks and nuns, who wear gauze masks over their noses and mouths to avoid swallowing even the tiniest gnat, and sweep the ground before them as they walk to avoid treading on the least living thing. They take five vows: not to kill, not to lie, not to steal, to indulge in sexual relations as little as possible, and to reduce their possessions to a minimum; they survive by begging, and spend their lives in pilgrimage to Jain holy places.

110 Jain nuns on pilgrimage. Girnar, Saurashtra, November 1987.

111 Jain ascetic. Shantinath Temple, Jhalrapatan, Rajasthan, August 1987.

There are two main sects in Jainism: the Shvetambaras, or 'white-garmented ones', and the Digambaras, or 'space-garmented ones'. The monk photographed at Jhalrapatan belongs to the latter group. He is entirely naked. Before him on the ground is the *kamandalu*, a wooden begging bowl; between his legs is his *chamar*, the little broom that he uses to ensure he does not step on any living thing, which is usually made of cotton threads but occasionally, as here, of peacock feathers. He is reading a sacred text. The practice of fasting is widespread among the Jains; in the case of this monk, it is a fast to the death, which ensures the passage of the spirit to nothingness and its escape from the endless cycle of rebirth.

112 A Jain monk. Miniature, Western India, 18th century. Private Collection.

He is wearing the *puttika* or veil across his mouth (to prevent him from swallowing and thereby killing any insects) and telling his rosary.

113 Kala Rudra. Miniature, Pahari, Basohli, 17th century. Sri Pratap Singh Museum, Srinagar, Kashmir.

This is one aspect of Shiva, who represents the universal power of destruction by which all life is terminated and from which all life springs. Shiva has two aspects – one terrifying, the other desirable; one immediate, the other transcendent. The terrible and beneficent aspects of the god are constantly interwoven, for his ultimate action is to kill death itself, and thereby to usher in eternal life. He is thus both the god of death and the source of life, that from which all creation springs.

In this miniature Shiva is portrayed as the leader of the yogis, with his third eye and crescent moon. His body is covered with ashes. His three eyes symbolize the sun, the moon, and fire. With them he can see the past, the present and the future. On his forehead, like a diadem, he wears a crescent moon, indicating that he is the lord of time, for the measurement of time in months or days depends on the waxing and waning of the moon. The tiger is the vehicle of Energy, the embodiment of the forces of nature, and Shiva wears a tiger skin as a trophy. His four arms stand for the four cardinal directions, thus symbolizing his universal dominion. The trident stands for the *gunas*, the three basic qualities, hence for Shiva's three functions as creator, preserver and destroyer.

114 Indian squirrels. Detail of a miniature from a *Babur-nama*, Mughal, 16th century. National Museum, New Delhi.

In his memoirs the Emperor Babur left us a vivid and occasionally humorous account of the people he had known, the flora and fauna of countries he had travelled in or conquered, and his joys, regrets, and mistakes. Of this little animal he wrote: 'there is also the rat known as "kalahri". It is said that he spends his life in the trees, from which he descends with extraordinary agility.'

115 Squirrels. Agra, December 1981.

In fact the correct form of the name, in both Hindi and Urdu, is *gilahri*; and the animal is a squirrel (*Sciurus indiens*) rather than a tree-dwelling rat.
Indian squirrels are engaging, friendly little creatures, who will even eat out of your hand: they are the tamest of all the wild animals in the subcontinent. They are only about 15 cm long, but their length is doubled by their plumy tail. They are everywhere, as much at home in town as in the country, swift as quicksilver, constantly uttering shrill staccato cries.
It seems impossible that Vishnu could have caught one of these creatures and kept it still long enough to stroke it and leave the mark of his fingers on its back, but that is, we are told, the origin of the squirrel's stripes. Miniaturists always had to set traps for squirrels before taking a few hairs from their tails to make the finest paint-brushes; in true Hindu spirit, they then released them again at the same spot.

116 Women performing *puja* around a pipal tree. Udaipur, March 1985.

The pipal, *Ficus religiosa*, is regarded as sacred by the Hindus, who believe that it shelters the god Vishnu. The women in the photograph have bathed and dressed themselves in silk before coming to perform their acts of worship. Each carries a little brass pot filled with water in her hand, which they carefully pour around the trunk as they circle clockwise round the tree; they then worship the *lingam* set up next to the tree, burning sticks of incense, making offerings of milk, butter and flowers, and chanting mantras.

117 Women performing *puja* around a pipal tree. Detail of a miniature, Rajasthani, Bundi, 18th century. Bharat Kala Bhavan, Varanasi.

The complete image shows Krishna watching the *gopis* (milkmaids) circumambulate the sacred tree.

118 Monkeys in a mango tree. Detail of a miniature, Oudh, 18th century. Baroda Museum, Gujarat.

These monkeys are playing with a turban they have stolen from a prince. They are langurs, often called 'Hanuman' after the popular monkey god, with silver-grey fur, black faces and long tails. The complete miniature shows a prince riding through the forest on an elephant. Indian monkeys are outrageously bold; they know they are sacred, and they do what they like.

119 Monkey with its young. Brindaban, Uttar Pradesh, March 1978.

This pair, playing with a garland taken from a temple, are rhesus monkeys or macaques, known in Hindi as *bandar*: they are the irritating *Bandar-Log*, the 'Monkey-people', of Kipling's *Jungle Book*. Like the langurs, they are sacred animals in India, not just protected but actively worshipped, and they exploit their privileged position to the full. Unlike langurs, who are vegetarians, rhesus monkeys will eat anything; their greed is insatiable, and they stuff extra food into their pouch-like cheeks. They may become aggressive, but usually they live in harmony with other animals and with man. Indeed, they live not only with but off man, raiding houses and temples, bazaar stalls, and even pilgrims' pockets for food.

120 Hanuman, the monkey god, at Girnar, Saurashtra, March 1989.

Hanuman's activities are recounted in the *Ramayana*, the great epic that was transmitted orally long before it was written down in Sanskrit five centuries before the birth of Christ.
The King of Ayodha was on the point of officially investing his son Rama with the title of crown prince when palace intrigues forced him instead to condemn the young man to exile in a forest for fourteen years. Rama set off with his wife Sita and his youngest brother, Lakshman. One day when Rama was away, Ravana, the demon king of Lanka, kidnapped Sita and carried her off to his kingdom. When Rama returned he set off, helped by the monkey king Sugriva and his army of monkeys led by Hanuman: they laid siege to Lanka, killed Ravana, and rescued Sita. When the term of his exile was up, Rama returned in triumph to Ayodhya, where he was crowned king and enjoyed a long reign. Hanuman was rewarded with long life and eternal youth, and served his master with unswerving

devotion. He is the perfect model of the servant of God.
Hanuman is presented as a refined and extremely learned individual, well versed in all the sciences, and his wisdom is matched by his strength. In sanctuaries and temples dedicated to him, he adopts a heroic posture, usually with a club in his left hand and Mount Sanjivini in his right. A bachelor and the embodiment of chastity, gifted with supernatural powers including flight and the ability to change shape at will, Hanuman is one of the most popular figures in Indian mythology. Among his various roles, he is the patron of wrestlers.

121 Hanuman. Contemporary folk mural on the wall of a little hermitage at Omkareshwar, beside the Narmada River, Madhya Pradesh.

122 Wrestlers exercising. Ayodhya, Uttar Pradesh, January 1988.

123 A wrestler with clubs. Miniature, Mughal, 1760, from the Small Clive Album. Victoria and Albert Museum, London.

This sort of training is still current in *akharas*, gymnasium-like places where men of all castes and religious persuasions between the ages of twelve and sixty come to exercise and to engage in traditional wrestling. The most important part of any *akhara* is a carefully set out area of loose earth, newly broken up and raked every morning, where the gymnasts practice wrestling. They enter this arena barefoot, like a temple, for it is holy ground; they tell a rosary and burn a stick of incense, sprinkling their forehead with the ashes. When they have finished practising, before the wrestling match begins they rub their bodies with earth mixed with healing mustard oil and curcuma.
Among the traditional exercises of the *akhara* are lifting the *jori* (a large round stone fixed to the end of a stick), doing press-ups, climbing smooth and knotted ropes, and wielding the large clubs known as *gadas*.

124 Wrestlers and men training with *gadas*. Glass-painting, Juna Mahal (Old Palace), Dungarpur, Rajasthan, 19th century.

In the 18th century, when the Portuguese, the Dutch, the French and the British set up establishments in India and inaugurated the golden age of the India trade, new products and techniques were introduced to the subcontinent – clocks and porcelain, wine and chandeliers, firearms and music-boxes, and, more surprisingly, glass-painting. As a novelty this was soon taken up by local artists, who found it easy to do, relatively cheap, and dazzlingly effective. They painted portraits to order for princelings, and images to be sold in bazaars near temples. Vigorous, naïve, robust, boldly drawn and brightly coloured, glass-painting was practised in a seemingly infinite variety of regional styles.

125 Wrestlers, Ayodhya, Uttar Pradesh, January 1988.

Traditionally, when they have finished wrestling the athletes are supposed to wait two or three hours before washing off the earth clinging to them from their exertions.

126 Wrestlers in the great *akhara*, Ayodhya, Uttar Pradesh, January 1988.

127 A pair of wrestlers. Miniature, Rajasthani, Jaipur, 18th century. City Palace Museum, Jaipur.

128 Sarmad, 'His Majesty the King of Sacred Eternity, May God have Mercy upon Him'. Detail of a miniature, Deccani, 1720. Galerie Marco Polo, Paris (by kind permission of M. Enrico Isacco).

We know tantalizingly little about this Sufi saint beyond the fact that he was a friend of Prince Dara Shikoh, the eldest son of the Emperor Shah Jahan, and that he was condemned to death by Shah Jahan's successor, Aurangzeb, for having dared among other things to go about naked in public. He was beheaded in Delhi in front of the Great Mosque in 1659. His tomb stands near the spot where he died: painted red, the colour of martyrdom, it is still an object of pilgrimage for those who venerate his memory, and who come to recite the three hundred or so Persian quatrains that he wrote, which are some of the greatest treasures of Sufi poetry.

129 Master One Thousand and Eight, a Vaishnavite sage. Great Kumbha Mela, Allahabad, January 1989.

This Vaishnavite master, photographed in his tent in the camp of the *bairagis* (Vaishnavite *sadhus*) during the famous 'Pitcher Fair', presents us with a parallel, or mirror image, between two spiritual traditions – Muslim and Hindu – and suggests, beyond differences in form, the essence that transcends and unites them.

The Kumbha Mela or 'Pitcher Fair' takes its name from the vessel of ambrosia over which the gods and demons fought during the churning of the Ocean of Milk (see caption 67). Drops of the ambrosia are be-lieved to have fallen in four places, subsequently regarded as holy: Prayag (Allahabad), Hardwar, Nasik and Ujjain. Every three years a great fair is held at one of the four places in turn, so the 'great' Pitcher Fair at Allahabad takes place only once every twelve years.

130 The letter *shri*. Miniature, Pahari, Kangra, 18th century. Chandigarh Museum.

This short mantra or invocatory formula, pronounced 'shreem', represents the goddess Lakshmi, consort of Vishnu, and symbolizes prosperity, good fortune, and magnificence. Lakshmi, the goddess of beauty, is also known as the Millionnaire.

'Shri' in everyday language is a form of address, just as 'Mr' is derived from 'master'.

As a mental formula designed to produce earthly riches, power, beauty and glory, *shri* is construed thus: *sh* represents the transcendent divinity of fortune, *r* signifies riches, and *i* satisfaction. The sound indicates limitlessness; its nasalization deflects pain.

131 A *pujari* (officiant). Temple of Sita Ram Mahavir Das, Maheshwar, by the Narmada River, Madhya Pradesh, January 1990.

The *pujari* is blowing into a conch shell during the *arati* ceremony. Performed five times a day in Hindu temples, this involves raising a tray laden with lamps fed by *ghee* (clarified butter) or camphor, accompanied by grains of rice, and rotating it around the image of the god. It is a symbolic offering of light, and as such it is also performed around a bridegroom or an important dignitary.

The *shankha* is a sea shell of which the tip has been cut off to form a mouthpiece. It was formerly blown in battle, but is now used only in temple rituals and in processions. With its spiral structure, starting from a single point and widening out into ever broader curves, it symbolizes the origin of being. Coming as it did from the sea, it is associated with the primordial Ocean, and the sound that it makes when blown is taken to be a reflection of the primordial sound from which all Creation has its being.

132 Priests blowing conch shells, accompanied by musicians. Detail of a miniature, Pahari, Kangra, 18th century. Bharat Kala Bhavan, Varanasi.

The complete miniature depicts the *arati* ceremony in a Vaishnavite temple, that of Jagannath in Orissa, where worshippers chant before the image of Jagannath, a manifestation of Krishna.

133 Krishna playing the flute, with Radha, his beloved. Temple at Galta, Rajasthan.

134 Radha, in a dramatization of the life of Krishna. Great Kumbha Mela, Allahabad, January 1989.

In the North Indian calendar, months begin on the day after the full moon, and are divided into two halves of fourteen days each – the 'dark half', when the moon is waning, and the 'bright half' when it is waxing. Throughout India, the month of Bhadon sees the celebration of the birth of Krishna. On the eighth day of the new moon children dressed as the young Krishna process through the streets, preceded by floats, elephants and horses. Vaishnavite temples echo to the sound of hymns and the divinely inspired stanzas of the *Bhagavad Gita*. The eleventh day of the new moon is Radha's birthday. Plays depict the most popular episodes in the life of the God.

135 A Jain woman. Jain temple near Jaipur, July 1987.

She is making the gesture of greeting known as *anjali mudra*, which corresponds to the traditional Indian gesture, *namaskar* or *namaste*. The two hands joined together vertically express wonder, adoration and prayer, without any need for words. The *anjali* is a greeting in the form of a flower, the lotus bud. Extended horizontally, its dualism recalls the intrinsic unity of the two halves of every human being, the masculine right side and the feminine left, which are to be reunited in a single nature. Extended vertically, raised above the head it is a sign of homage to the gods; at face level, to the *guru* or teacher; and at breast level, to Brahmins. It is the noblest form of greeting in the world, rich with a thousand virtues and a thousand secrets, a complete yoga in itself.

136 *Begum* (great lady) holding a flower. Miniature, Deccani, Bijapur, c. 1625. Jagdish and Kamal Mittal Museum of Indian Art, Hyderabad, Deccan.

This high-born and ample lady, like the Jain woman in our photograph, exudes a strong personality with great generosity of spirit.

137 A *mukhalingam*, or combination of *lingam* and human face. Indian bronze, 18th century. Private Collection.

Shiva, the manifestation principle, can be perceived only through his creation. The *lingam* or phallus, which is the source of life, is one of the forms through which he can be depicted and venerated. The *lingam* is the most sacred symbol of the person of Shiva, the great inseminator: it is associated with the female sexual organ, the *yoni*, and is usually represented in conjunction with it.

In a Shaivite temple, the *lingam* is always to be found at the centre of the innermost sanctuary, fixed in the ground, a massive object, ranging from the stylized to the highly realistic.

The *mukhalingam* form expresses the close connection that exists between the human face and the *lingam*. Yogis believe semen should not be released: through the discipline of *hatha yoga*, it is controlled and redirected vertically to the upper *chakras* (located between the eyebrows and at the top of the head), thereby transforming sexual energy into mental energy.

138 A Hindu *guru*. Allahabad, February 1989.

An archetypal image of the power of latent energy masterfully held in check.

139 *Puja* (offering) in honour of Shiva. Bheraghat, by the Narmada River, Madhya Pradesh, January 1990.

Every morning throughout India, from the Himalayas to Cape Comorin, millions show their devotion to their favourite deity in prayers which may be performed in the open air, in a temple, or at home.

The man seen here is a Brahmin, identifiable by the sacred thread across his chest. The ritual required of Brahmins is always extremely complicated. Clad only in a traditional *dhoti* or loincloth and the sacred thread, he is pouring water on the *lingam*. Next he will anoint it with sandalwood paste, sprinkle it with flowers or hang a garland of flowers around it, and burn one or more sticks of incense.

140 A raja adoring the Shiva *lingam* in a temple. Detail of a miniature, Rajasthani, Jodhpur, 18th century. Private Collection.

141 The bathing ghats of a little town. Miniature, late Mughal, Oudh, 18th century. Baroda Museum, Gujarat.

In India, the banks of rivers and of sacred lakes or pools are faced with stone steps forming stairways that make it easier for pilgrims to reach the water. These flights of steps are known as *ghats*. Sometimes they are on such a vast scale that they recall the tiers of seats in a Roman amphitheatre.

The ghats are the focus of intense activity in the morning and evening, the prescribed times for ritual bathing and religious observance. More mundanely, they serve for people to wash themselves and their clothing. In large cities the ghats extend for miles along the river and serve specific functions. Raj Ghat in Varanasi (Benares), for instance, is used by washermen, while Rana Ghat is the preserve of Muslims, and Manikarnika Ghat is used only for cremations.

142 Bathing ghats. Udaipur, Rajasthan, December 1987.

143 Woman praying to the sun. Miniature, late Mughal, 19th century. Chandigarh Museum.

144 Woman performing the same prayer. Dwarka, Saurashtra, November 1987.

The worshipper stands facing the sun, arms raised and palms turned inward. He or she then recites certain mantras, and calls upon the great giver of light and life to all living beings. This woman has gathered water in a *lota* from the river beside which she is standing; she raises the little brass pot as high as possible, and then slowly pours its contents back into the river. Alternatively, water may be scooped up in the worshipper's cupped hands, which are then parted to release it in a thin stream.

145 Women emerging from the bath. Detail of a miniature, Rajasthani, Bundi, 18th century. Allahabad Museum.

The complete miniature shows Krishna coming across a group of bathing *gopis* or milkmaids.

As long as India has existed, men and women have bathed in her rivers and identified with her gods and their manifestations or *avatars*. Among these is Krishna, who can be venerated under any of a number of forms corresponding to the various stages of his life – infant, child, adolescent, warrior, husband or lover. Every individual, regardless of his spiritual attainments or the language he speaks, can address the gods in the certainty of being heard. All approaches are equally valid, for all spring from a single feeling, love.

In Krishna's own country, it was the custom at the beginning of the winter for the milkmaids to pray to a particular goddess for her help in finding the perfect husband. Secretly, each prayed that she might marry Krishna. The *gopis* then plunged into the waters of the Yamuna to purify themselves, and performed a ritual in honour of the goddess, whose image they modelled out of river silt.

146 Two women dressing themselves after bathing in the Narmada River. Nemawar, Madhya Pradesh, January 1990.

147 A beautiful woman holding a mirror. Sculpture, Mathura style, Kushan period, 1st or 2nd century AD. From Sanghol near Chandigarh. Sanghol Museum, Punjab.

This *yakshi*, or nymph, holds a mirror in her left hand and with the index finger of her right hand points to long, crescent-shaped scratches made on her cheek by her lover.

The eighteen-hundred-year-old beauty, as moving as she is marvellous, with her broad rounded hips curving up to her perfectly formed breasts, embodies the distinctive voluptuousness of Indian women that has been praised by poets over the centuries: 'From the tips of her breasts, rounded like jars, she blossoms' – thus Jayadeva in the *Gita Govinda*, or 'Song of the Cowherd' (Song VII).

148 A *gopi* emerging from the Narmada River, January 1990.

Elsewhere in the same song, we read: 'On the domes of her tumid breasts, [Krishna] spreads gleaming musk; he takes beads and arranges them as clusters of stars, and with his nail he marks the outline of a crescent moon'

149 Sarus cranes. Near Kanpur, September 1987.

150 A *dhobi* (washerman) helping a sarus crane to take flight. Miniature, Mughal, 17th century. Bharat Kala Bhavan, Varanasi.

The sarus crane (*Sous Antigone*) is said to be native to India and to be the oldest of all living birds, and the largest of all that can fly. It is a symbol of long life and fidelity: it mates for life, and that life may be as long as that of a man.

151 A woman bathing. Galta, Rajasthan, November 1966.

152 An *apsara* (nymph or female divinity). Sculpture, Hoysala period, 12th century. Temple of Belur, Karnataka.

Do sculpted bodies exist to illustrate poetry, or do poems exist as descriptions of them? In his *Gita Govinda*, which is exactly contemporary with the *apsara* at Belur, Jayadeva cries: 'Your breasts are so beautiful, and sweeter than the nut of the wine-palm tree – will you let them go to waste, unused?'

153 The moon god Chandra in his chariot drawn by an antelope. Miniature, Rajasthani, Mewar, *c.* 1700. Private Collection.

The moon god projects the beneficent influence associated with that planet – good health for one's family, good harvests, prestige, and royal patronage. In Indian tradition the moon is associated with the elixir of immortality and life: it is the cup filled with the ritual liquid *soma*, which is drained by the gods and miraculously re-filled. In yoga, *soma* means sexual energy. The moon is a cup full of semen that has been mastered and transformed into energy, representing the power of the mind.

154 A couple on the beach. Dwarka, Saurashtra, November 1987.

The couple that we photographed playing in the blue waters of the Arabian Sea seemed to us archetypal: they were Shiva and Parvati, Shiva pursuing Parvati, Man and Woman. In the words of the poet, 'Believe me, it is as difficult to keep quicksilver still in the palm of your hand as to make yourself master of a young wife.'

155 Shiva and Parvati bathing. Miniature, Pahari, Chamba, early 19th century. Chandigarh Museum.

Just over two years after taking the photograph, we found the miniature to match.

156 A Hindu funeral. Detail of a Company painting, 1866. India Office Library, London.

157 Cremation on the banks of the Gogra. Ayodhya, Uttar Pradesh, September 1987.

Calling out the name of Rama as it passes, the funeral procession reaches the cremation site beside the river. The body is set down on the bank, and purified by being immersed in the water up to the knees. Then it is laid on the pyre, on a bed of cowdung cakes, and the eldest son lights the fire with a flame brought from the family home.

The cremation takes three or four hours. It is a sacrifice to the god of fire, Agni. The organs of the deceased are enjoined to return to their original source: sight to the sun, *prana* (the breath of life) to the air, *manas* (the intellect) to the moon, and the body to the earth. It is a moving farewell, in which the body is consigned to the cosmic elements that gave it birth.

Once it and the wood are consumed, the ashes are gathered up and cast into the river.

158 Women weeping over a body. Miniature, Pahari, Basohli, 1765. Bhuri Singh Museum, Chamba, Himachal Pradesh.

The miniature forms part of a series illustrating the *Ramayana*: the women seen here are lamenting the death of Rama's father, Desharatha.

159 Funeral procession. Coonoor, Tamil Nadu, March 1966.

The deceased, eyes closed but face uncovered, is carried shoulder-high on a bamboo litter to the cremation ground amid a crowd of relatives and friends. Before that, the body had been wrapped in a cloth – white for a man, red for a woman – and placed on the bier to the accompaniment of the mantra *om*.

160 The goddess Kali. Miniature, Rajasthani, Kishangarh, 18th century. City Museum, Jaipur, Rajasthan.

The name 'Kali' comes from *kala* – time, in the sense of duration. Kali represents the power of time by which everything is destroyed. Kali inspires terror in the beholder; but she is also the creator, the Great Mother.

Shiva is Brahma, the Absolute and Unnamable, who assumes all forms and performs all actions: he is therefore shown prostrate, like a corpse. Kali is his *shakti*, or energy; energy cannot exist in a vacuum, and that is why she is shown standing on the body of Shiva. While she represents the destructive aspect of divine power, Kali also connotes the state that follows the ending of time – the everlasting, boundless night of peace and joy.

161 Kali made flesh. Pushkar fair, Rajasthan, November 1966.

On the occasion of great religious festivals and pilgrimages, the gods of the Hindu pantheon and their *avatars* mingle with mortals to enhance and exploit their faith.

162 An old horse attacked by crows. Miniature, Mughal, 17th century. Topkapi Library, Istanbul.

This scrawny horse, with all its ribs showing, is a pitiful sight; two crows feed on its open sores, while a dog has seized on one of its hocks.

163 Water-buffalo carcass and vultures. Rajasthan, March 1978.

A crowd of vultures means a dying or dead animal: they will wait for hours until the victim has expired and then throw themselves onto the corpse, roughly jostling for position, uttering raucous cries and whistles, fighting for a particular morsel and feeding on it until they are glutted, before flying off and leaving the remains to the dogs. Their function as scavengers is recognized as an advantage.

In India birds figure largely both in fable and in real life. The vulture (*Gyps bengalensis*) is associated with the earth and with the sky – with earth, because the ancients believed that hell was ruled by the king of the vultures, and with the sky, because as the mythical Garuda, the half-bird, half-man vehicle of Vishnu, the vulture symbolizes the sun itself.

164 Hindu *sadhus* (holy men). Detail of a miniature from a manuscript of the *Mahabharata*, the great Hindu epic, 17th century. National Museum, New Delhi.

These *sadhus* are *kanphats*, distinguished by their earrings, which may be of bone, glass, wood, jade, horn or metal, and of any size. A *sadhu*'s ears are pierced in a painful operation that forms part of the initiation rite, and large earrings keep the lobes distended.

Hair is a symbol of power in all cultures. The hair of *sadhus*, known as *jata*, is remarkable for its length, its thickness and its consistency. They never comb it, and they rub it with a milky juice derived from banyan twigs that makes the hair grow more vigorously and gives it the appearance of thick woolly strands matted together. They wear this mane in one of two basic ways: hanging loose over their shoulders, or tied up – either in a great bun on top or at the back of the head or wound round to form a crown, the *jatamukata*.

165 A *sadhu*. Pushkar, Rajasthan, November 1983.

166 A *naga sadhu*. Girnar, Saurashtra, March 1989.

This Shaivite *sadhu* is completely naked, and his matted hair hangs down over a body that is entirely covered in ashes. Those ashes come from the ritual fire that he keeps perpetually alight; they represent the ashes of a funeral pyre, and as such symbolize the *sadhu*'s complete renunciation; and they also allude to the action of Shiva, who reduced the universe to ashes and then covered his body with them.

The trident or *trishula* is the symbolic weapon of the Shaivites, who on occasion made real use of it to defend their faith, and this *sadhu* stands with it as though he were on parade.

From the trident hangs the Shaivite *damaru*, the little hourglass-shaped drum that is a reminder of the one with which Shiva accompanied himself when he danced the cosmic dance and created the world. It is played by flicking it so that two lead pellets on the end of strings hit the two membranes.

167 Shaivite *sadhus*. Company painting, Patna, 1827. Galerie Marco Polo, Paris.

168 Fighting *sadhus*. Detail of a miniature from the *Akbar-nama* (Story of Akbar) of Abul Fazl. Mughal, *c*. 1596. Victoria and Albert Museum, London.

The complete miniature shows the Emperor Akbar watching a fight between two rival bands of *sadhus* at Thaneswar, near Ambala in the Punjab.

169 *Sadhus*. Allahabad, January 1989.

As we described at the beginning of the Introduction, we came across a scene electrifyingly like that in the miniature during the last Great Kumbha Mela of the 20th century: these two thousand naked *sadhus*, heading in a chaotic crowd towards the Ganges, were photographed from an observation platform.

170 An archer. Detail of a relief illustrating scenes from the *Ramayana*, on the Hoysaleshvara Temple, Halebid, Karnataka, begun 1235.

The warrior has an elaborate headdress or hairstyle.

and strings of *rudraksh* beads decorate his arms and ankles.

171 A Shaivite *sadhu*. Girnar, Saurashtra, February 1988.

Twenty-three years after we had taken the photograph at Halebid, we came across this *sadhu* garlanded with *rudraksh* beads and suddenly understood the eight-hundred-year-old relief. *Rudraksh* means 'tear of Rudra', and, as Shiva gradually became assimilated with Rudra, 'tear of Shiva'. Rudra, the most powerful of the three chief gods of Hindu mythology, is the destroyer, and his power is manifest throughout nature – in fire, that burns; water, that drowns; wind, that sweeps away; and man, who kills. The name is explained as meaning 'He who weeps', or 'He who makes weep'. Rudra is the Lord of Tears.

It is said that after a battle against the demons in the course of which three cities were destroyed Shiva shed tears for the loss of life; his tears fell on the ground, and where they fell bushes sprang up that produced the berries known as *rudraksh*. The *rudraksh* tree (*Eleocarpus ganitrus*) is found chiefly in Nepal and in South-East Asia. Its browny-red berries, which are cleaned and polished before being threaded into rosaries, have varying numbers of cells or *mukhee* which determine its value and represent particular qualities. Shops catering for pilgrims usually sell rosaries made of fake *rudraksh* berries. The real ones are highly prized by Shaivite *sadhus*, who by telling their beads to the accompaniment of specific mantras believe that they are enveloped by good cosmic vibrations.

172 A yogi telling his beads. Miniature, Mughal, 1630. India Office Library, London.

173 A Vaishnavite *sadhu*. Great Kumbha Mela, Allahabad, January 1989.

Shri Mahant Omkardas Katthya wears his hair in long strands wound round his head in concentric circles; in addition he has the distinctive sign of the followers of Vishnu on his forehead. This usually consists in a U shape representing the footprint of the god; the vertical line in the middle stands for Shri, or Lakshmi. Arranged as here, they indicate membership of the Ramanuja sect, founded in the 11th century. For the followers of Ramananda, a 15th-century Vaishnavite saint, the two vertical sides of the U honour Rama and his brother Lakshman, while the central line honours Sita.

174 'Glorious Sun'. Miniature from a *Kalpa Sutra* (a Jain holy text), Western India, 16th century. Museum of Fine Arts, Boston.

175 Winter sun. Near Kanpur, January 1988.

Only in a thick mist such as you find in the Ganges plain in winter could we point the camera directly at the sun. What we needed next was a mirror: we found a perfect sheet of water. The resulting monochrome image exudes a sense of mystery akin to that of the miniature, which is preserved in the American museum where the great Ananda Coomaraswamy worked for years. A sentence of Coomaraswamy's has long stayed in my mind: 'He who wants to bring back the riches of India must take within himself the riches of India.'

NOTE Throughout this book, the word 'India' is used in its broadest historical sense, to include Pakistan.

Acknowledgments

We would have liked to mention all the people who, over the past twenty-five years, have in a thousand and one ways helped us better to see, to understand, and to portray India. Among them, our special thanks go to:

– Hervé de la Martinière, our publisher at Nathan in Paris, for the interest he has always shown in our work, an interest that led him as far as to come and see us in India

– Benoît Nacci, our *guru* in matters of layout, who patiently introduced us, year by year, to the complex world of book production

– Roger Sabater, Christian Arrivé and Jean-Pierre Di-Meglio, and their team, for the fine quality of the photogravure and printing of the present volume

– all the librarians, museum curators, and private collectors who generously cooperated with us on our project

– Jacques-Yves de Rorthays, Michel Tallard, and the technicians of the Vieux-Campeur

– Pierre Rietzler, president of Wild-Leica France, and the whole Leica team

We are grateful to our Indian and foreign friends throughout India, both for their hospitality and for their kindness:

– in Ahmedabad: Amit Ambalal, Chantal and Achille Forler, Shikha and Renuka

– in Allahabad: Rustom Gandhi and his wife, S.S. Mishra

– in Ayodhya: Yogi Raj Munishwara Nand Das

– in Bombay: Aruna, Lance Dane, Jahangir Gazdar, François and Christiane Nicoullaud, Orlando Norowha, Adrian and Hira Steven

– in Chandigarh: Daniel and Melissa Massat

– in Delhi: Sudhir Anwar Aggarwal, Brigitte Freyche, Bernard, Alexandre and Hélène Larose, Mukundan, G.B. Singh, Swaran Singh and his son Manender

– in Hyderabad: Sarfaraz Husain and all his family, Chumki, Dilkash and Sahira

– in Jaipur: Bannu, Mohan Lal Gupta, Kumar Sangram Singh, Sunny and Brigitte Singh

– in Jodhpur: Dilip Sunara

– in Lucknow: Nawab Mir Abdullah, Pradeep Kumar Misra, Rocky and Rekha Mohan and their family

– in Nathdwara: Dwarkalal Jangid and his family, Chiranjeev Lal Sharma and B.L. Sharma

– in Srinagar: Bashir and Zahida Butt and all their family

– in Tonk: Malika Aziz-u-Zamana Begum Sahiba, Shaukat Ali Khan, Mirza Rafiullah Beg and their family

– in Udaipur: Shriji Arvind Singh Mewar and Kanwrani Sahiba, Miguel A. Arregui and Gopal Kapoor, Bina, Deepak Dutt, Chris Deagan and Indu, Bara Lala and Chotta Lala and all their family

We would especially like to thank Achille Forler for his help in choosing the extracts from the *Upanishads*, of which he made a new translation from the Sanskrit for the French edition of this book.